ENDING THE BLAME GAME

I0161345

ALSO BY THE AUTHOR

What's Wrong With Me?: A Girl's Book of Lessons Learned, Inspiration and Advice

What's Wrong With Me? Reflections Journal

END NG
THE
BLAME
GAME

SINGLE BLACK FATHERS ON
RELATIONSHIPS

DAREE ALLEN, MS

Kharacter
DISTINCTION

Atlanta, Georgia

ENDING THE BLAME GAME

Copyright © 2014 by Daree Allen. Printed in the United States of America. All rights reserved. No part of this publication may be reproduced, stored in a retrieval system, or transmitted by any means—electronic, mechanical, photographic (photocopying), recording, or otherwise—without prior permission in writing from the publisher, except by a reviewer, who may quote brief passages in a review.

Published by Kharacter Distinction Books, 4355 Cobb Parkway, Suite J185, Atlanta, GA 30339.

Ending the Blame Game is a work of nonfiction, but the author has changed the names of the people depicted in the stories herein.

This book contains information gathered from many sources and personal experiences. It is published and sold with the understanding that neither the author or the publisher is rendering any legal, accounting, or psychological advice. The author and the publisher disclaim any personal liability for the advice and information presented herein. Although the author and the publisher have prepared this manuscript with diligence, careful to ensure the accuracy of the information presented, they assume no responsibility for errors, inaccuracies, omissions, or inconsistencies herein.

ISBN: 978-0-9837-4554-9

LCCN: 2013914086

CONTENTS

PART I: OUT FOR SELF

PART II: WE'RE NOT THE HUXTABLES

PART III: YOU AND ME AGAINST THE WORLD

CONTENTS

FOREWORD

We live in a day and age where information is readily available with a few strokes of the computer keyboard. Still, many people are unable to decipher the real and true from the fake and falsified. Often, the media has been at the forefront in the perpetuation of the fake and falsified.

When one's psyche is presented with repetitious images, whether true or false, it will begin to accept them as truth. The black community has been indoctrinated, and in many cases, intimidated by media images. It has been inundated with symbols of: 1) a male that is an irresponsible, sex-crazed brute who cannot commit to his family, 2) a female that is a hyper-sexual narcissist who is unable to love, trust, or appreciate her man, and 3) a child that cannot learn and has no hope of a future. In essence, the relationship of the black male, his woman, and his family has been incrementally sabotaged by FEAR: *False Evidence Appearing Real*!

I created an affirmation that now serves as one of my mantras. When faced with amazing odds, I tell myself, "Where there's hope, there's possibility, and where there's possibility, there's life!" Daree Allen, MS provides hope, presents possibility, and speaks life! She has a true passion to see the life and personal psyche of the black male positively edified, and his voice clearly heard.

In *Ending the Blame Game*, Daree has created a blueprint for success that is guaranteed to empower, encourage, and inspire the requisite communication that will ultimately lead to the emotional and mental liberation of a people. This dynamic book also gives the black woman insight into the complex emotions of her man. As a result, relationships will be healed, families will be unified, and the truth will indeed set us free!

— Myles W. Miller
International Speaker, Author, Coach, and TV/Radio Personality
Detroit, Michigan

INTRODUCTION

"Don't fight to win. Fight to understand."
– Paul Carrick Brunson

The rates of unmarried/divorced couples and single-headed households in the black family unit are higher than ever. The voice of the black male in American society is muffled and skewed by the media. Black males are looked upon as a "throwaway species," with little value to add to families, Corporate America, and the larger society. There is a strong, general distrust that can only be overcome by education, enlightenment, and communication.

The comparison between Mother's Day and Father's Day is a no-brainer. As moms we get a lot more fanfare in the black community—as well we should if we hold it down for our families as the sole heads of household. But what about the men who own up to their responsibilities and just need a little love and respect?

I'm a single mother and my ex-husband is not very active in his daughter's life. But many men are not like that. I don't believe that in a disagreement, there must be a winner and a loser. The mentality among some couples is that one person has to be right and one has to be wrong. Am I here to take sides? No—that kind of thinking influenced the title of this book.

Ladies, brothers want us to know that the problems in our relationships are not always their fault. Sometimes we just don't want to hear the truth, even when we've asked for their honesty. They want to share their side of the story. Like me, they want to explore themes such as: What would it take for us to stay in a relationship, and make it stronger? How can we come together and have each other's back without animosity and distrust?

I've taken a small cross-section of Black America—people that are really going through it—not celebrities or rich folks. Men that

---

want to be with us, ladies! But why can't we—men AND women—just get it together? Every disagreement does not have to have a winner and a loser. Why can't we just end the blame game altogether?

HOW THIS BOOK WAS BORN

My cousin Rico gave me the idea for this book. In the summer of 2011, he reached out to me and our conversation lasted over four hours. Rico had been separated from his wife, Karyn, for a few years and wanted to move on with his life. At the time, he had a girlfriend and an apartment in town, while his wife and three kids lived in their house. She also had a boyfriend for a time, as I heard it. We talked, laughed and shared stories as if we were old friends from high school.

Rico told me about his life with Karyn, whom he started dating in high school, their separation, what he wanted for his children, and what he ultimately wanted for himself (to be loved and be happy). He expressed frustration, concern, and showed me his heart toward his children and love in general.

Our fathers are the oldest of our grandparents' seven children and were best friends until his father died in the early eighties. Our grandparents died in the 90's, two years apart. Their marriage wasn't always smooth, but they loved each other and were committed to each other till the very end.

As a single mother with no prospects, I couldn't help but think, *Why can't I find a man like that?* Rico insisted that I write a book from the perspective of single men who want love: "You like to write books? Well, let me tell you about the next book you need to write." I was in the production stages of my first book, and he was already giving me my next project: relationships from a male point of view. Sure, we've already got that covered by the likes of black celebrities like Steve Harvey, Hill Harper, Rev. Run and Tyrese... but what about regular people? And single black fathers?

I'm a divorced single mom who lives in Atlanta and works from home. My desire is for a long-lasting, committed, loving relationship with a regular dude who is stable and has enough love in his heart for me and my daughter. And from what I hear, there's lots of single men who want the same.

So what's the problem?

Well, if you haven't noticed, romantic relationships among black couples, like many relationships, can get complicated pretty quickly. Whether it's sex, money, children, or communication issues, we don't seem to truly understand or agree on how to start or maintain a healthy relationship, and remain committed to keeping them strong. We also have a lot of lingering resentment, distrust, and unresolved hurt from past experiences and relationships.

In this book, we're going to eavesdrop on some conversations with real men, almost all of whom are single, divorced, or remarried with children. The scenario for this group of men is that they grew up in the same town (some of whom went to the same high school), and reunite during Memorial Day weekend. In reality, most of these men have never met, but I've combined their real-life stories and experiences to show a common thread between how black men think about women, and their desire for real love and family with their beloved black queens. Their honesty exposed their personal struggles with their own demons and issues with their upbringing. A few admitted their trifling ways with women, along with a desire for monogamy. Others admitted a lack of knowledge in choosing a suitable mate to begin with. All clearly love and take care of their children.

After each conversation, you'll see how relationship experts weigh in on the issues discussed with takeaways, tips we can use, and insights we can reflect on and apply to our relationships.

THE "CAST"

Ladies and gentlemen, I'd like to introduce you to the following "cast of characters" featured in the conversations of this book, as well as the experts who comment on the conversations. The men's stories as you see them here are as they were told to me in their own words. I've changed their names throughout this book (except my "cuz"), but we all know these fellas, because we have brothers, cousins, and partners just like them. Their descriptions below include their metropolitan areas and marital status, and most have attended college, but I purposely omitted their occupations to eliminate early prejudice and classification on the basis of their job and/or income level. (Refer back to this section as a reference if you lose track of whom is speaking.)

~NEVER MARRIED~

Name: Donnie
Age: 33
Status: Never married
Children: One son (age 9)
Current Location: Okinawa, Japan

Name: Joe
Age: 39
Status: Never married
Children: One daughter (age 8)
Current Location: Dallas, Texas

Name: Lamar
Age: 41
Status: Never married
Children: Two daughters and one son (ages 6 to 15)
(One child from current relationship; two children from previous relationship)
Current Location: West Palm Beach, Florida

Name: Tommy
Age: 37
Status: Never married
Children: Two sons, one grandson (sons' ages 7 and 17)
Current Location: Virginia Beach, Virginia

~*MARRIED*~

Name: Cory
Age: 35
Status: Newlywed
Children: One stepdaughter, one son (ages 8 and 14)
Current Location: Newark, New Jersey

Name: Derek
Age: 41
Status: Remarried
Children: Two sons (ages 15 and 19)
Current Location: Dallas, Texas

Name: John
Age: 47
Status: Remarried
Children: Two daughters (ages 2 and 18)
Current Location: New York, New York

Name: Luis[1]
Age: 37
Status: Married
Children: One son (age 6)
Current Location: Los Angeles, California

Name: Quincy
Age: 41
Status: Remarried (One divorce with no children, one child from previous relationship, two children from current marriage)
Children: Two daughters and one son (ages 6 to 13)
Current Location: Atlanta, Georgia

---

[1] Luis is Mexican, but I included him in this book because of his insights and experiences shared with his wife and best friend (Michael), both of whom are black. He was considering separation at the time of our interview.

~*SEPARATED*~

Name: Michael
Age: 37
Status: Separated for seven years of 10-year marriage
Children: Three boys and two girls (ages 8 to 16)
Current Location: Los Angeles, California

Name: Rico
Age: 42
Status: Separated for four years of 21-year marriage
Children: Twin daughters and one son (ages 18 and 7 respectively)
Current Location: Dallas, Texas

~*DIVORCED*~

Name: DJ
Age: 40
Status: Divorced; would like to marry again someday
Children: Three sons (ages 6 to 19)
Current Location: Fort Worth, Texas

Name: Pete
Age: 48
Status: Divorced
Children: Three daughters (ages 16 to 25)
Current Location: Fort Worth, Texas

Name: Spencer
Age: 34
Status: Divorced (previously married for 5 years)
Children: N/A[2]
Current Location: New Orleans, Louisiana

---

[2] Spencer is the only person in this book who is not a parent. I made an exception because he shared powerful insights that I believe will enlighten you.

Name: Terrence
Age: 42
Status: Divorced (previously married for 9 years); would like to marry again someday
Children: Three daughters (ages 6 to 13)
Current Location: Richmond, Virginia

Name: Tony
Age: 28
Status: Divorced (previously married for 4 years); would like to marry again someday
Children: One daughter (age 9)
Current Location: Fort Worth, Texas

MEET THE EXPERTS

My panel of expert commentators are experienced in family and relationships coaching and counseling, and have been featured in many national publications. In subsequent chapters, you will see their comments on various conversations, based on their expertise. Here's a little background:

MELISA ALABA is a Licensed Professional Counselor and life coach. "The Vision Coach" is the founder and Executive Director of Vision Works Counseling and Coaching. She has over 12 years of experience as a counselor and cognitive behavioral coach from a Christian perspective. She is also a presenter and trainer, and has also studied and practiced mindful meditation since 2008.

EZECHIEL BAMBOLO, JR. ("ZEKE"), also known as "The Firstborn Son," is an author and speaker who focuses on the strategic importance of family legacy. He was born and raised in Liberia, West Africa, as the first son of African-born missionaries and teachers. Ezechiel coaches youth, men, and families, focusing on the biblical concept of the firstborn son as a familial conduit for the stability of the individual, family, culture, and the nation.

JACK A. DANIELS is a best-selling author of five books including *I Need a Wife...Where are the REAL Women?* and *The Man's Handbook for Choosing the Right Woman.* He is a psychotherapist, syndicated columnist and international speaker. He has appeared on media outlets such as BBC, Fox News, CBS, NBC, ABC, Esquire, and DateDaily, and is one of the leading authorities for giving advice about passion, purpose and relationships.

RACHELLE MILLER, JD is an experienced family attorney, minister, and relationship coach who is dubbed "The Relationship Manager." Rachelle's ministry service began in Greensboro, North Carolina and continued to Houston, Texas at Lakewood Church, the largest church in the U.S. Rachelle holds degrees in Law and Journalism, and has studied marital, pastoral, and women's counseling at Liberty University seminary, and is a member of the American Association of Christian Counselors. Rachelle is currently based in Atlanta, Georgia.

DR. IVAN PAGE, MSW is a social worker, family therapist, and Associate Professor at Albany State College in Albany, Georgia. He specializes in the black family and relationships. He's been quoted in *Ebony* magazine and other media outlets.

TRINA PROCTOR is an entrepreneur with a private practice in the cities of Smyrna and Marietta, Georgia. She is a licensed psychotherapist and counselor, who has served in the social service field for 14 years. She is also certified as a Psychiatric Rehabilitation Practitioner. Currently she is an adjunct faculty member at the University of Phoenix. She is also a member of the American Psychological Association and United States Psychiatric Rehabilitation Association. Her main goal is to educate "to reduce the negative stigmas attached to mental illnesses" everywhere.

EBONY A. UTLEY, PHD is an expert in popular culture, race, and romantic relationships. Her writing has appeared in a variety of publications including *Black Women, Gender, and Families*, *Huffington Post*, and *Marriage and Family Review*. Dr. Utley is an Associate Professor of Communication Studies at

California State University, Long Beach and lectures at universities across the country.

RICHARD MAURICE SMITH, PHD is an Assistant Professor of Sociology and coordinator of the Master of Science program in Public Administration at McDaniel College in Westminster, Maryland. He focuses on the sociology of religion and the sociology of race and racism. He has presented at professional conferences on a variety of research topics, and liberal and conservative Protestant views of sexual morality in the U.S. Dr. Smith has taught sociology classes in race and racism, the historical significance of race in American society, American ethnicity, and cultural anthropology.

LET'S GO

Black families are suffering from broken relationships; what will it take for us to come together? With this book, I hope to start conversations and dialogue that will lead to healing in our relationships. Other goals for this book include:

- Improving communication

- Fostering more compassion, patience and understanding

- Giving solutions and ideas on how to improve our relationships

- Encouraging more love and less strife in relationships

- Reducing divorce statistics among blacks and go back to being married for a lifetime like our (me and Rico's) grandparents

Now, let's open the door and see what real men have to say about love, longing, and life as a single black father.

PART I:
OUT FOR SELF

CHAPTER 1:

IT WAS OVER BEFORE IT STARTED

The cast arrives in their hometown on a Thursday afternoon for a Memorial Day weekend celebration; some have brought their wives or girlfriends on the trip. Some of the guys played basketball earlier that day. Later that evening, a bigger group of the fellas meet up at a sports bar without their significant others. Beer and nachos are on everyone's minds as they sit around a large table and a server takes their orders. After congratulatory shout-outs on the game, the conversation turns to women.

MISUNDERSTOOD

RICO

Women know a good man from a bad one. Who will be more responsible? They put more pressure on the good guy than the bad one.

SPENCER

Women always say, "There are no good men out here." Well, most men are good. The good guys I know are the ones who get the raw deal. They get mistreated, cheated on, and they turn bad and treat people like they don't care. We bow, we bend, we care—and a woman takes advantage of it. So my attitude is, "I'll just enjoy having any woman I want."

♟ GOOD GUYS AND BAD BOYS ♟

MELISA ALABA: There's some validity regarding the discussion about "good guys" and "bad boys." It happens. With women who chase bad guys, there's something in them that desires that, hasn't matured, or they feel that they don't deserve the good guy. Maybe they've experienced life without a father figure, or their expectations weren't met, like when a father promises something but never showed up. Or maybe they don't know what a good marriage looks like. So there's an idea that you have to work hard to get and keep a relationship. If someone treats them well, they get suspicious and think, *What does he want? Why is he so nice to me?* She's familiar with the bad guy: "I've got to mold him, I've got to chase him." That's just what they know. I don't think good guys have it harder; it's that these men may have more insight and that's why it seems harder. They want to make sure things are fair so they may go to court. A working man wants to be involved with his children. If you were a thug, a woman may not take you to court. You're cognizant of the situation and are thinking about it, while the thug doesn't really care that much.

DR. PAGE: Whether a woman wants a "bad boy" or man is acting like one, depends on where they are in life. Women pick a bad boy because he's fun, exciting and entertaining, not boring, and that applies to the sex, too. Bad boys let the woman get her orgasm first to make her think, *He cares about my needs.* He'll do different sexual positions instead of just regular, traditional, missionary positions. But at some point, women who deal with them long enough come to realize that they can't trust the bad boys.

The bad boy has excuses: he had a hard life, and his father wasn't there... if only if he had support and love, he'd be a better man. So the woman delays her success by loving (mothering) him, or she lets him down or leaves him behind.

PETE

I gave my friend a kidney, but yet I'm a selfish motherf—er or an assh—? Nah. We know we're good men and we want to be good. We want to be hit in the eye—tell us the truth.

DJ

The problem is that there's no real communication. Women say, "Just tell me the truth." So I try to tell the truth: "I'm at Saltgrass [restaurant] with Rico." Response: "Uh, why you there?" So I'll just lie so I won't have to argue with you. You try to do the right thing though...

QUINCY

We can't be responsible for anything in this society, so you couldn't say, "Maybe I'm doing something wrong." Nope. Instead you say, "Ah, that's not it, you are looking at it wrong." As long as we're fighting, and I'm busy trying to fix you, defend myself, and protect myself, we're not moving forward.

TERRENCE

Some people focus on "If this doesn't work," but that's the wrong attitude; instead they should put the focus on "What can I do to make this work?"

JOE

You can't win for losing regardless of what you do, so take care of yourself.

RICO

They think you tryin' to hurt them from the jump.

JOHN

Men really don't leave, but they may want something on the side. Women leave.

RICO

Sometimes our attitude is like, "You can't tell us sh—!" We know everything? No we don't.

SPENCER

The heart of a black man is that when we're in a relationship or the prospect of one, our morals change. When I was 15, I would go up with my boys and we'd go to house parties, dances, and football games. We'd talk about the girls we were interested in. That conversation has not changed over the years.

JOHN

It's always interesting to read blog comments on black websites and YouTube: "That's why black women ain't got no man," or "Black men are lazy." Negative comments just perpetuate.

Black men don't respect black women and vice versa. That breeds distrust and disrespect. It makes us look at each other differently. Because of distrust, we get offended when someone is not on our program.

I went to a house party for a friend's baby's birthday party and I hadn't shaved my mustache, so I'm lookin' like a brotha. One woman looked at me like, *What are you doing here, nigga?* There is constant judgment of each other.

LUIS

I think when black women see me, they think, *How bad can he be?* because I'm not black. But they don't know that I'm the biggest racist in the world. I hate all races equally. *(They all laugh.)*

(The server delivers two bread baskets. Rico and Luis take a roll from either basket and pass them.)

SPENCER

When you are dealing with a person that is genuinely unhappy, any happiness you share is just for that moment, and tomorrow it's all forgotten. I remember when I went to Old Navy to get a gift for my ex-wife. I'm unaccustomed to giving gifts—it was reaching for me. She disregarded the gift and didn't acknowledge my effort, but I couldn't admit how much it hurt. There was no pleasing her.

Sometimes she would sabotage happy times by questioning something or saying something that would ruin the moment. At this point, I know I can't make anyone happy. I can put a smile on your face, but inner peace and joy doesn't come from another person.

RICO

(Still chewing)

Women be like, "Why don't men get Valentine's Day gifts?" Start making us think about it and get *us* some gifts. Why is it always about the woman? Why can't a man come home and get pampered like the song "Cater 2 U"?[1]

JOE

I know at this rich Christian school in North Dallas, there's women whose husbands might be scandalous but they got a mil in the bank; they don't care if their hubby smashes.[2] When there's a bunch of zeroes behind a comma, you'll put up with more.

DJ

Today's black woman is totally different from back in the day. It's a totally different era. You can get caught up though. I know one dude was messin' around with this woman and she got

---

[1] A song by Destiny's Child.
[2] Has sex with another woman.

pregnant. He got that bread. He killed the girl and found out later she wasn't even pregnant. His wife found out, and he didn't want his wife to take him to the bank.[3] He was comfortable having fun on the side, and their kids was taken care of.

JOE

When you get laid off, women think you're sorry. Women by nature look at men as the providers. Women want that Jodeci fantasy—"Love You for Life"—but you have to be working together toward a common goal, not just waiting to be rescued.

LUIS

When I relocated from L.A. to Atlanta, it felt different. I'm used to taking care of things, but now my wife was taking care of me. She had a job there, and I didn't.

DJ

Women just want to know that they can be taken care of.

JOE

(*Nods in agreement*)

Yeah, they need security. But you know Chilli?[4] You can't pick your life.

DONNIE

We all need to stop talking about what we want and just be a little more open-minded when it comes to what we want in a mate.

---

[3] That is, sue for alimony if they got divorced.
[4] Chilli is one-third of the 90's R&B group TLC, and had a reality show in 2011 called *What Chilli Wants*. In that show, she was looking for love, and had a long list of requirements for her ideal mate.

DEREK

Here's my charge to men 30 and up: You should have an idea of what's important and what's not. You ought to be able to say whether hooking up with this woman will get you to your next destination in life. What do you plan on doing with your life? If you have a goal, you will have a woman. In the movie *I Think I Love My Wife*, Chris Rock's character said: "You can lose a whole lotta money chasin' women, but you lose women chasin' money." Have your priorities straight. Money represents security. Men want be appreciated and women want to be covered and protected. If we provide, they will appreciate us.

JOE

At first the women I dated had to be black. Over time, I switched and went to white women exclusively. It's a lot easier to talk to white women because they don't make a big deal out of every little thing. Last week I went on a date with a black woman who was irritated that I was five minutes late for the date. That bad attitude—I call it BWA[5]—happens a lot. The white women are more easygoing—you can't generalize, but I see white women as more easygoing, without all that anti-man stuff.

TONY

Some women are too damn strong and need to relax and sit the f— down. Some females don't know their place. I don't believe in hitting a woman, but some females cross the line and get in your face when they argue. I believe Rihanna started that fight with Chris Brown.

---

[5] Black Women with Attitude.

LAMAR

Sometimes the black woman's attitude is just wrong to me. It's borderline nasty sometimes when they get angry or don't like what you have to say. I don't feel the black women treat black men the way we should be treated—especially those of us who do the right thing by taking care of our families and holding down a job. But when it comes to the ones who don't have any concept of manhood, black women treat them better. It's like nice guys finish last and the bad guys get the glory.

DONNIE

Some women are too independent for their own good. They need to learn how to sit back and be a lady. You don't have to show all your strength all the time. I like a woman to be vulnerable... subservient. Don't get me wrong, I love a strong black woman, but don't be on no bullsh—. Some of y'all tryin' to be intimidating. I absolutely love black women but they get on my last f—ing nerve, and they're so hard to deal with. I have always seen myself settling down with a black woman, and having a beautiful queen, but sometimes I find myself doubting my own theory and wonder about being with a white woman.

JOHN

At 21, I learned that if I acted like an ass, I got plenty of girls. I didn't give a sh—. I'd tell them up front "I have bad intentions" or "I have a girlfriend" even if I didn't, and they was still with it. But after a while, I didn't want to deal with multiple women anymore. It got tedious and tiring. AIDS was becoming prevalent and I got nervous.

SPENCER

Most men love to provide for kids and make their women happy. But if a woman has never seen it before they don't know how to receive it.

LAMAR

They don't cater to us the way we should be catered to. And when they see a black guy with a white girl, they wanna know why they got the good black guys—but they don't always do the right thing by them.

TERRENCE

The infighting that we have not learned to conquer causes us to look to other races. The way black women speak to us makes my friends wanna marry another race. It's used as a power tool.

JOHN

(Shaking his head and lightly taps Terrence on the shoulder)

Yo, I know white girls and there's no way you can tell me that a white woman is easier to deal with than a black woman when they're mad. I remember when a friend of mine had a white girlfriend who got mad at him and told the cops he raped her. Has a black woman ever taken you to court for sexual misconduct?

I've had a lot of friends that had problems with black women and their attitude now is, "I don't mess with sisters no more," but that's a cop-out. If we look back, the reason why we're so dysfunctional[6] is because we were enslaved for 400 years. That's the crux of it. It's the big elephant in the room that we try to ignore. You have to look back in the past to gauge where all these attitudes are coming from. Black women tell their friends, "Ah girl, you need to get yourself a white man." Why not say East Indian man or Asian man or Latino man? We've been conquered by them. That goes back to slavery, but we don't never wanna deal with it.

---

[6] As a race.

♟ THE "ANGRY BLACK WOMAN" ♟

DR. SMITH: The angry black woman is a stereotype and based on a perception. Is she angry, or strong? Is she not willing to be taken advantage of? Is she assertive? You don't get that same view of men.

PETE

I started an interracial relationship when I was 10, and the girl was 13. That was when I had my first sexual experience. In high school, I won an award for computer programming but didn't get the scholarship. The guy I taught was white and he won. So getting with women may be what I perceived as trying to get a better opportunity. I enjoyed the conquest of getting white women to get back at the men. But I've been with Samoans, Filipinos, Thais, and Germans... If I had completed college I might have found more intelligent black women that I would have dated, but I left and went into sales at 21. I learned the game in business on Wall Street—it's still the game.

The pearly white woman I live with now is controlling and possessive and crazy, and I allowed it. I've been with her for seven years. She's a nice lady, and I wanted to make her life better... I was in rescue mode. I bought her house, paid her bills, and paid for her kid's car.

I know it's not fair that I've been living with her for seven years—I've deceived her by stringing her along. But she hasn't come to my expectations. She's not quiet. She is possessive, and wants to know what I'm doing every minute.[7] She's needy—I can't

---

[7] Pete's girlfriend called him seven times during his 90-minute interview with the author. He did not answer any of the calls.

---

go out to the car or smoke a cigarette in front of the house without her asking me where I'm going. I'm thinking, *Do you want me around because I'm a man? Or because you don't wanna sleep alone at night? You don't treat me like a man.* I'm still with her because I'm comfortable in her house, but I'm preparing my credit, and I'm getting a roommate so I can move out. I'm just here for her for a season. God preordained it.

LAMAR

I wasn't looking for a girlfriend at the time that I met Jennifer. I grew up not paying much attention to racial differences, so it never bothered me that she was white. A lot of black women didn't like me enough to want me for a relationship. I was introduced to Jennifer in college by her black roommate, Trina, who was a residence advisor on campus. The following week I saw her in the campus bookstore and we spoke briefly. A couple of weeks later, Trina started seeing my best friend. She approached me in the cafeteria at school and told me Jennifer liked me. I was like, "Word?" I stayed off campus, but they came by later that day and we started talking. I was still cautious at first because I wasn't looking for a relationship. After we got together, a lot of my black female friends at school were mad about it for a while and gave me the cold shoulder, but my family and friends were cool about it. We stayed together for 14 years and have two daughters.

(A server delivers their food, and everyone starts eating.)

SPENCER

I admire the way white men run their homes and treat their women. They're attentive to their women. If black women could ever get over their devout allegiance to exclusively date black men, black men would take notice. Many black men are not capable of holding down the fort. We need something to wake a brotha up—but right now we don't have to because we got it made.

TERRENCE

Black men also are dedicated to black women and that's natural because that's who you are.

PETE

I don't know... is satisfying your ego the path of least resistance as far as getting with light-skinned women as a trophy? Or is it substance? What is my substance and my spirit? My grandmothers are the strongest women I know. One is black and Cherokee, and the other one is Cherokee French.

TONY

I love black women to the death, and especially natural women. [8] I like their attitude and their "for sureness," like, "Nigga, you know you like this." Black females have more confidence and strength than some other races because of what they've gone through. My inspiration about women in general is that they're humble and strong. They'll take nothing and make it into something. I have to applaud a woman who will take a dude who has nothing and make a relationship into something that's worth having.

> I have to applaud a woman who will take a dude who has nothing and make a relationship into something that's worth having.

JOHN

It's a new phenomenon; a lot of young black women are not as nurturing as they used to be. They've been through so much it makes them a bit masculine because they can't rely on

> They've been through so much it makes them a bit masculine because they can't rely on black men.

---

[8] Women who wear their hair in its natural texture.

---

black men. Some of these women are committing more violent acts, and going to jail more often these days.

JOE

It's a cultural thing. A lot of times I think black women are stronger than white women because they have to be; often they're the sole provider.

JOHN

My teenage daughter has only seen me with two women other than her mother, and one of them is my wife. You can't have just anyone around your kids. My daughter thinks I'm great and ethical.

RICO

How are kids affected by broken families and their parents' relationships? If they grow up seeing an unhealthy relationship, they get used to it, so it's acceptable and normal and they become immune to it.

DJ

God made men stronger for a reason; it's all our fault for a lot of the stuff goin' on now. I had to raise my kids because that's how my daddy raised me.

JOHN

Young people don't have any training[9] and they're not prepared. We say things to our sons like, "You gonna be a lady killer," or "He's gonna be a heartbreaker." And then they do that—they give girls diseases.

---

[9] For relationships.

If a child's parent doesn't go to college, there's no pressure for the child to go. We make some stuff okay because we do it. I can't preach to my kids about drinking or smoking if I'm doing it. And then they're constantly being fed messages of disrespect from music and TV. Some of these kids are having oral sex at age 11.

DEREK

The show *Cops* is an example of how they[10] are making money off of inner city issues—not suburbia. It's all about money, and they've got different priorities.

QUINCY

(Rolling his eyes)

People love to watch people act like idiots on reality TV. Who wins? The network execs.

DEREK

Saggin' spelled backwards is niggas. In the 80's we had this complete switch in mindset when NWA and gangsta rap came out. It became cool to be locked up and kill people. There was a total swing in music; feeding our kids with a huge media component—emulating rappers and celebrities—letting the TV be my parent and "entertainment." What happened to riding bikes, using BB guns, PlayStation, and playing outside?

Grandmas are 45 now. There's no accountability—the mindset is, "I wanna be my kid's friend." There is no village raising the child, no manners being taught to assist women coming home with groceries, and so on.

---

[10] The media.

♟ Parenting and Media Literacy ♟

Melisa: When two people conceive a child, the pressure of the baby greatly affects the relationship, how it changes, and the demands the baby puts on the parent. What also makes things harder is the higher rate of unmarried couples with children. When you're not married, it's easier for couples to separate; married people have to work together a little longer.

Dr. Utley: Critical media literacy is key to helping parent our kids. We have to accept that we live in a mediated world. We can't protect our kids from it all, but we can help them to interpret it so that they do not passively accept ideologies. It takes time and patience to engage our kids about all the ideas they're exposed to, but the more we know what they're thinking, the better we will be able to communicate with them and interrupt problematic concepts.

Dr. Page: My 14-year-old daughter likes Drake and Rick Ross, so one day we sat and watched music videos and talked about them—how they demean women, singing about their butt and other body parts, and the way the women in the video were dressed. It was a non-judgmental environment; my wife and I just point things out and reflect our values. We tell our daughters, "Here's what we believe, how we should dress, act, and speak." Kids try to be like everyone else they see because of peer pressure. I think parents should sit down with their kids and analyze music and dances, and the how the women dressed in the music videos are showing their breasts and butt.

Dr. Smith: When it comes to reality TV and other shows, understand that the media reacts to society and reflects it back to us, but the media can also be used to inform society. It may tell us, "This is how a man or woman should act; these are examples of good or bad relationships; this is what's proper," and the shows we watch give us advice.

Young people see hip-hop culture and are influenced by it: hip-hop says how they should be; hip-hop tells them what it is to be black, and how they should act and dress.

JOHN

We're asleep on the job. We need to instill something in our children other than what a singer is doing or a reality TV star. It's gonna take each individual to do their part. We tell girls "Don't get pregnant... Stay in school," but they're watching *Real Housewives*. Give them something they can use! How can you be a parent but can't teach your kid sh—?

CHAPTER 2

THE MAN IN
THE MIRROR

I t's early Friday morning. Spencer, Luis, John, Rico, Cory, Terrence, Quincy and Lamar are preparing a boat to go fishing. Actually, most of the guys are standing around while Quincy, Cory and John do most of the work. Luis asks Spencer how his folks have been.

Am I Worth It?

SPENCER

I wanted validation from my father but never got it... always felt like I was never good enough and always had something to prove. Situations with women where they didn't appreciate my efforts just reinforced those feelings. My father groomed me to be this way.

TERRENCE

I used to have self-esteem issues... I wouldn't look in mirror. I was diagnosed as depressed, but I'm against medication. Now when it comes to labels, I don't feed into them and they don't bother me because I know it's not me.

LUIS

(Takes a drag on a cigarette)

Growing up, I wasn't taught how to be satisfied in my own skin. I can't exist inside my own head—I would explode. I gotta do something with hands and my mouth.

I used to try to keep up with the Joneses. No one told me it was okay to make a mistake, so I'd run and try to do something to cover it up. I was in and out of county jail in L.A. I'd start to take calculated risks, and ask myself, "Can I do another two years?" But once you start losing your loved ones, your health, and your freedom, you wake up. I'm not going down that road again.

♟ Men and Their Feelings ♟

Jack A. Daniels: Getting to the core of our feelings and the root of them is a mystery to everyone. I say that men are like turtles: we're hard on the outside, soft on the inside, but we'll stick out our necks for what we believe in. Once you do get inside, we are soft and mushy. But once we get into a relationship with someone we love, and they hurt us, we don't want to stick our necks out again.

Believe it or not, men are more emotional than women. Studies have shown that boys are more emotional than girls (saying "gimme," crying, and being whiny). Boys become trained to be harder, firmer, and tougher as we grow. So we shield ourselves from showing emotions we used to as a kid. "Real men don't cry?" Or, "Are you really feeling that way about her?" It's looked at as demoralizing to be moral. It's humorous in a certain sense because you have so many guys who don't understand who they are. Their identity is a strategy for their life. They can't tell a woman what they need, want, and require.

However, men will express their feelings during intimate moments. We have so much pain in our lives and sex is pleasure. We pursue sex for the pleasure and relief from pain. Before and during sex is probably gonna be the first time he says he loves you. But it's not that he loves you—he loves the feeling. You're also gonna have a lot of pillow talk. He doesn't have any critics around so he can express himself freely. But once you're out of the way, those feelings go away.

Women have the power to tap into that soft spot whenever they deem it necessary. You can teach him how to tap into that soft spot under our hardened shell. Be sensitive and gentle about it. We lack it but we crave it. We're afraid to admit that we need women in our lives to love us.

TERRENCE

I struggled for years with the decision of whether to leave my wife. Afterward, I questioned myself every day about whether I made the right choice. I felt like I had let her down, let the kids down, and let down a whole race of people. But it was a courage thing. It was a personal thing and I wanted answers. One night I went to church and the preacher's message was that we need to take care of ourselves, see what we need to fix in our lives, and reach success in whatever way we define it. So when I left that night, I decided to go on a journey to find Terrence. The old Terrence and the new Terrence fight a lot! It's more about self-talk than it is actions.

CORY

Society sees us men as big, brawny warriors that don't need help, but that's not the case. We don't always have a model for how to be good fathers.

QUINCY

(Pauses from loading equipment on the boat)

Women say things like, "You're a man, you should know," or "You're a man, figure it out." But what if I was never taught or shown what you're asking me? How do I know what to do if it was never modeled for me?

(Gestures for Lamar to help him lift something)

SPENCER

We can't go around and say, "This is what a woman is supposed to do." But they say it to us and I have to be in a certain role. How do you engage someone who's in transition? They want the freedom to be who they want, but we can't.

> **Women want the freedom to be who they want, but we can't.**

LAMAR

Man, these ladies out here gotta understand that some of us are hardworking, take care of our kids and give them everything we never had. Some of us are loyal when you do right by us even when you don't give us the support we need. But as soon as something goes wrong, that's when we try to flip the script and our attitude changes toward you. It goes downhill from there.

RICO

Women don't think they have to support their men. I'm an entrepreneur and CEO of an entertainment company. I struggled to build this company with no support from my wife. I remember when she said, "I ain't takin' care of no man." But I'm not just a man... I'm your husband. She said, "I didn't ask you to marry me; you asked me to marry you." Now she wants me back because she found out her man was married,[11] and because of my increased income. But you can't just talk to me any kind of way.

SPENCER

I got divorced because my ex-wife didn't support me. When we got married, I started writing for a

> **I got divorced because my ex-wife didn't support me.**

black newspaper in New Orleans. She said, "Sometimes I feel like

---

[11] They are separated and dating other people.

---

you care more about your writing than you do me." So I stopped writing.

In my freshman year, I went to register for school about one and a half hours away from where I lived. On the way home, I was pulled over by the police and detained for 13 hours on the charge that I robbed a bank!

TERRENCE

What?! That's crazy, man.

SPENCER

Yeah... they took my fingerprints, interrogated me, impounded my car and took it to Baton Rouge. When I called my wife to tell her what happened, her response was, "We were supposed to go to the movies. Do we still have time to go?"

Then another time, at my dad's funeral, I was in a family photo. On the way home, she had her face frowned up, mad because I didn't invite her to be in the family photo. It was so selfish!

I didn't know that I needed support. I thought that because she loved me that would be enough. The truth is, she didn't have it to give.

> I thought that because she loved me that would be enough.

JOHN

My wife supports me, man. I was heartbroken when I didn't have any money. But she'd say, "We're gonna get through this." I had the world on my shoulders, but she made me feel like I could conquer the world.

(All of the guys get on the boat and take off.)

Don't Talk to Me

DEREK

With all this instant messaging, texting and tweeting going on, there's nothing deep—no in depth conversations... people are breaking up on texts, arguing on texts. This microwave society needs to get back to the basics and fundamentals. Let's sit and talk to each other. Court a woman. And blacks don't want to go to counseling—it says, "I admit that I'm weak and I need help—I have issues."

CORY

(Throws down his fishing rod)

A lot of men have no relationships or friends they can talk to except at bars or somewhere talking about sports.

RICO

When we go to bars, it's like, this is our spot. We don't just go to get drunk and BS; we ain't that dumb. We talk about sports and everything just like women, and give each other advice. It's like our counseling session over a pitcher of beer, because we don't wanna be at home.

♟ The Way Men Socialize ♟

Dr. Smith: There's a societal conception that attacks our masculinity if we're talking about something deep, as if you're not really a man if you're sharing what's on your heart.

For men to connect with women, there has to be something going on other than just talking. We could be talking while working on a car, or at a sporting event.

SPENCER

It doesn't do any good to go seek mental health. My healing process was a lot of crying while dealing with the things my mom allowed me to see in her relationship with my dad for 30 years.

TERRENCE

I'm vocal with my feelings and understand things that happened in the past. I talked about it for comfort before; now it's about change.

RICO

We as men can all do this—talk... We all need therapy and counseling, but we try to be so hard like we pimps and gangstas, but women run this world, trust me. When we get hurt, we don't know to express it so we act out, and try to suppress our anger. We're born to be protectors and don't wanna seem weak when a woman breaks our heart.

> When we get hurt, we don't know to express it so we act out, and try to suppress our anger.

We're private people and don't want anyone in our business. But it's not a bad thing. We might need to deal with issues from when we were raised that affect our relationships as adults.

JOHN

(Takes a sip from his beer bottle)

When you go to a therapist, they want to know your history, so they can determine what's making you the way you are today. But for us it's that everything right now is like, "You're an assh—, or you're a b—"... But were you molested? Did you have issues with one of your parents not being there? Realize that just as you grow and learn, our parents were growing and learning as they raised us.

DJ

People should be open to counseling—be open to communicate. I dated a girl and we went to counseling. The therapist gave us tools to help us support each other. You want to marry someone and you're not willing to understand how they were raised? Do they have trust issues, mental issues? Other issues from the past? That's why I can't get with Steve Harvey[12] because he's not looking deep into the situations of why we act the way we do.

It causes problems in marriage if your mate was raised differently; that's why you gotta be open to the counseling, so you can look deeper, and your business stays in the household. You don't seek nonprofessionals—it leads to gossiping.

♟ Therapy ♟

Dr. Utley: These guys raise salient points about the importance of counseling. Counseling is not just for couple relationships but also for families. There's nothing about becoming a parent that automatically makes you a good one. People should also be more open to family counseling and parenting classes to help rear the kind of kids they want to see. For some blacks, counseling is anathema because they attend churches that encourage them to pray about their problems and have faith without seeking professional help. Also, many counselors are white, and lots of people of color are hesitant to tell all their business to a white stranger. Besides, there are cultural differences that sometimes make white counselors ineffective.

Jack A. Daniels: If your mind's not right, and you want to change your life, change your mind. How else can you get ahead? You can't always walk and talk your way through it.

Melisa: TV is making it easier for African Americans to get counseling or coaching and takes some stigma off of pursuing it. We're getting better at seeing there's not something wrong with

---

[12] Refers to Steve Harvey's book *Act Like a Lady, Think Like a Man.*

us. A lot of men come to my practice that just want someone to talk to.

Dr. Page: Black men don't go to therapy, and we're probably wrong. But we don't think we're crazy, so we're not going. We'll talk to a friend before we go to a licensed therapist.

A lot of people use their friends as a sounding board for their issues, but you have to pay attention to the personality of the friend you confide in. It's a good idea to have all kinds of friends. You need friends that will keep it real and keep it "100" with you, as well as friends who will be there for you unconditionally. If you're talking to someone who knows you well, you can ask "What do you think I'm doing wrong? How can I improve on this behavior?" Be ready for an honest answer: "Your temper is too quick." You want to talk to people who will keep you grounded. You want to come to common ground.

If you want to go to counseling and you don't want to talk to a stranger, you can go to your pastor—that's acceptable in the black community. The key is, who do you trust—a stranger, who is more objective, or your pastor? It's your choice.

TOMMY

(Rubbing his beard)

When I have to make decisions or something is bothering me, I deal with it on my own. I deal with everything myself. If I'm dating someone at the time, I'll talk to them about what's going on. I say things to get them off my chest, but I don't rely on anyone where I can say, "What do you think about this?" No matter what situation I'm going through, even if I talk to someone else about it, I've pretty much decided on my own how I will handle it. I may even call a professional—like a lawyer—to get their expertise, but I'll make my own calculated decisions, and I do so at my own pace. I'm not vindictive—I take my time with things like that.

♟ Put Your Hands Up ♟

Jack A. Daniels: It's extremely hard being a man. We don't like to talk about it, but it's there. "I know I'm where I'm supposed to be, but I just can't get there because of _____." I want more but I can't get more. That adds stress to our lives. When we have children out of wedlock, we get frustrated with responsibility, which adds a degree of denial and blame, which can turn into anger and depression.

We've been reared with a sense of hardness. We don't acknowledge it; we just keep going. High blood pressure, alcoholism, substance abuse—these are some of the results when we numb ourselves from the pain of being present in a place where we don't want to be. A lot of people don't understand the moodiness or roller coaster. You can get help to regulate those levels of moodiness, but because of our pride and ego, we won't raise our hands for help. You know those old cop movies where the cop catches a guy and says, "Freeze! Stick 'em up!"? You have to say "I surrender." Surrendering is the most vulnerable position because you've got your arms in air, and everything is exposed—your chest, heart, and vital organs. We're afraid of that vulnerability; admitting it is seen as a sign of weakness.

People walk around thinking that emotional wellness and health are not a priority, but we have to dispel those stigmas and stereotypes in the black community. It's okay to be vulnerable and say you don't have all the answers, or that you don't know all the strategies. Simply say you don't know. What you don't know can hurt you so much more than what you do know.

> What you don't know can hurt you so much more than what you do know.

Ladies, here's how you can help a man who's feeling depressed or having some emotional stress in his life:

1. Get him to keep a journal or write things down somewhere.

2. Encourage him to pick up a new hobby or resume an activity he enjoys. Men communicate better during activities—we don't sit down on the couch, cross our legs and talk. We have to be doing something before we will talk (driving, basketball, etc.). You can do it with him if you want him to talk to you, or he can do it alone in his own space to process things.

3. Don't be so quick to get an answer from him. Men process things slower than women.

4. Make subtle suggestions about being around other men (for example, at sports bars or sporting events) so he'll be more comfortable talking things out or venting.

CORY

Social services are usually dedicated to women and single mothers. At my job, we have the best comprehensive programs for men in Newark. Men are receiving attention and developmental training in our program. These men have been beaten up by life; many of them were incarcerated, separated from their family, or had no parents. These are the kind of issues that hold us back.

Our community is dealing with the massive issue of abandonment; 70 percent of the men are gone[13] because of abandonment or incarceration.

---

[13] Absent from black households.

If you have limited education and experience, you can't get a job. It's difficult to achieve anything with just a high school diploma, so we offer GED programs and vocational training in construction, landscaping, and other skills, or they can go to college. It's a full-service menu that men can participate in and enhance their skills as fathers, men in the household, and their families.

No man is an island. This is a brotherhood; a place where men can have conversation and unload thoughts on what's on their minds. Seldom can these men freely express themselves, so when they come to this program, it's like getting a therapy session.

Take this for example: A 37-year-old man is in our program, and he has no job. He's been on his own since age 12; his foster father sexually abused him, and he's been hustling since age 17. He said he's been involved with a 45-year-old woman now for six months. He says loves her and is faithful to her. Then he mentioned that "other women support me," so I questioned whether he was really faithful. I said, "Did she give you lunch money today?" and that triggered an angry response. I had to calm him down and get him to see that he's looking at his girlfriend as if she's his mom in a way.

♟ Picking a Mate like Your Parent ♟

Melisa Alaba: Having real trust with each other in relationships is a big issue. Some people either knowingly or unknowingly label their partner as their parent (like the man that Cory mentioned); they label something as a negative even if they didn't see it. This often happens when a behavior from their partner triggers something their parent used to do when they were a kid. Or, they take one situation and label it based on their past personal experience. Even after the offending person says "I'm sorry," the other person can't accept it. There's too much quick judgment, unforgiveness and unwillingness to see a situation differently.

CORY

Every 12 weeks, we run an eight-week program. During orientation, we test their commitment. Does the applicant stay for the full day, or have excuses on why they are late or have to leave early? We also do one-on-one interviews before placing them in jobs. Funders don't care about the sob stories. If the person we place isn't committed to the job, it makes us look bad.

In the program, we cover employment skills. We do an educational assessment of reading and math levels, and participants improve two grade levels while they're with us. We have doctors, life coaches, and job coaches do assessments and career inventories. We find out who they live with, their criminal history, and address health issues.

We also teach basic life skills—simple things like when to go to bed and when to wake up. They don't have the skills to know, like scheduling their transportation to allot time to get to work, or call their supervisor to let them know if they are running late. We talk about parental responsibility and relationships—how do you select a girlfriend or a wife? What characteristics, background and upbringing should you look for in a mate? They don't think about it until it's too late... when a child is conceived and they feel stuck.

We have attorneys that can petition the court when there's an unrealistic child support order, and get the court to acknowledge their bills and income and grant temporary leniency while he is at new job to wait until his wage increases. They get discouraged by the mounting child support debt, and then if the child's mother says, "You can't see your kid because you didn't pay," it becomes a vicious cycle. We also offer counseling about how they can work together to get along for the sake of their child.

I tell these guys that you don't have to be in love with your children's mother to have love for her. We have a responsibility to our kids. I also tell them that if you're the smartest guy in your crew, then you have a problem because you

> **If you're the smartest in your crew, then you have a problem.**

don't have anyone to guide you, mold you, or tell you when you're messing up.

♟ Being a R.E.A.L. Man ♟

Zeke: I can tell what kind of man you are from the kind of life you lead.

Are you prepared to change your circle to become healthier for yourself? Read some books and get some knowledge. Put yourself in a core of people who are healthy and knowledgeable. Think ahead of time and be strategic about what you want, and how many kids you want to have.

If you need a place to grab wisdom and get clarity, seek out a small group at church or a men's retreat. You can form a group where you can have prayer and get accountability. If you're not gonna live what you say, your accountability partners will kick in, and help bring you back to your focus. You need to a place to go where you can be R.E.A.L.. [14]

R - Reject Passivity

E - Engage with God

A - Accept Responsibility

L - Lead Courageously

---

[14] R.E.A.L. is from Dave Wilson, Co-Founder of Kensington Community Church in Troy, Michigan, and the long-time chaplain of the NFL Detroit Lions.

SPENCER

(Chuckles)

When you get out of jail, most family members welcome you with open arms like you just graduated from college.

CORY

Well, we've graduated 400 men from our program. Every February, we give awards for the men who've completed any of our four classes that year. The graduation is an event where the men in the program can celebrate with their family and friends—not because of coming home from jail, but from a real accomplishment.

Headed for Self-Destruction

While Luis, John, Cory, Quincy and Lamar head back to their hotel rooms or families' homes to chill, the rest of the crew decides to check out their old barber shop around the way, where Tommy and Cory are waiting for their turns in the chair. They greet the owner with a hug and a pound, and start talking about their past and present self-destructive behaviors.

PETE

(Looking at the TV, shaking his head)

Cocaine empowered me falsely and disassociated my responsibilities. It was a type of power. People wanted it; I named a price. I could spend $1,000 in a titty bar and not give a sh—. That was the cheese to please among some of the sleaze.

I met a stripper who would bring girls home with her and call me—we'd get wild together. I'm not braggadocios—I was just lost.

JOE

I wanna do things my way and I don't think about the consequences of my actions... but then I worry about it later. I've had resilience and been able to bounce back. But I'm stubborn. I was once out with a Puerto Rican girl, and I ended up telling her something like, "If you don't like it, you can leave." So she left, and I knew I was wrong, but I didn't wanna call her. I wanted her to call me and apologize. It's pride. And I have this attitude that *they all come back*. But she didn't.

TONY

This chick I know got a dude that wants to be with her, but she wants me. It's like fatal attraction. It's lust. We're genuine friends but there's no future for us. She kissed me. If I was 20, it would have been on and poppin'. Some women misinterpret kindness for something more.

I hate playin' the game. I wanna be a little more straightforward. My lust is my downfall—I have sex with women too soon. And then the woman says, "I wanna be with you for the rest of my life."

PETE

I met my ex-wife when I was a male entertainer. I had a 12-pack. She is Mexican, and kinda looked like Appollonia with the gloves, the hats and all that. But for six months to a year, she wouldn't talk to me. One day I was working, and she and her white friend that liked me—she looked like a mini Dolly Parton—got drunk and very sexually aggressive with me. I felt like I was a piece of meat to women. I decided to take them home. In the middle of foreplay, we were on the couch, one on each side with alcohol and sexual freedom granted. But "Dolly" couldn't handle my endowment. My biggest regret is that I allowed "Dolly" to be a springboard to "Appollonia" because all I thought about was getting my nuts off—I was 21 at the time.

JOE

I'm not at that maturity level where I can just consider a woman attractive and leave it at that—most men can't do that. Planting that seed—"Look at her ass..."

I'll admit my biggest regret: I still wanted to hang out and bring chicks around my boys. My mentality was, I'm a weekend dad because I wanted to kick it and smash chicks. But my daughter's mother was willing to try to make it work.

TONY

Lust is like a disease. I want to love a woman for real, but the halter tops, fishnet stockings, music videos, shaking ass—I fall for the diversions. My granddaddy told me, "When you ain't gettin' none, you might have to pay for it." I do.

RICO

We 40 years old... sex is sex, and we've had enough sex. Don't you want love?

JOE

My uncle said that your life is not about how many chicks you ran up in. When you're 68 years old, you want to have a family. You want to leave a legacy. When you die, you want people to say, "That was a good man."

PETE

I still have internal conflict from seeing very passionate clips in my mind of my parents in parties, embracing and having sex; smells and freaky stuff going on all around me—adults cheating and swinging. On the other hand, in the late 60's and 70's things are hush hush and they don't talk about those times. I don't know if that programmed me to be how I am now. I'm wild and crazy. I'm promiscuous and free. But I don't think it messed me up as a person—I am what I am.

Families with strong relationships should be rooted in you to help you be able to have one. I'm not blaming anyone—it's just an observation. Knowledge is learned and gained from past experiences. It's hard to be successful without a mentor.

JOE

As men, we need to get the attitude of "I wanna be out there" out of our system if we want to be happily married. Until we get content and change our mentality, it's not gonna happen.

RICO

If I'm always the one giving, and I don't ever get anything back, I can't keep messing with you—I'm tired! I'm tired of playing with women like that. I finally found a giver, but I don't know how to accept it and sometimes I push her away because of it. I'm in danger of messing up something I've wanted my whole life.

TERRENCE

I'm very confident and don't have any expectations. Before I had an elevated level of expectations. I used to want my love interest to be my BFF, honor me, understand the road I've been down and be there for me when I'm feeling stressed or frustrated. I wanted to be loved, be a good listener, and to lead! But all the while I was dating, I thought, *I still love my ex-wife and would take her back.*

JOE

I've thought sometimes to myself that I'd rather be alone for the rest of my life than be with a big girl. But the things I'm doing will cause me to me alone for the rest of my life. I don't wanna be that short fat dude with a vest on, with a Jheri curl and slack shorts doing the electric slide with 22-year-olds, poppin' like ReRun,[15] or wearing a Tony Soprano sweat suit when I'm 50. I want to be happily married.

♟ Depression vs. Diversions ♟

Zeke: Some men in this chapter expressed a desire to leave a legacy, but feel frustration from not having fathers in their lives. Some had sentiments such as, "I should have this by now." But not all who seem depressed actually are.

---

[15] From the TV series *What's Happening Now!*

There is a difference between depression and confusion. It could be a mental disturbance versus a lack of understanding and uncertainty. Men who lack excitement in life and being fulfilled in their relationships will have a lack of energy that can lead to depression.

The progression of media has led to isolation. Media impacts us and causes us to redefine certain things in our lives. The slave era, World Wars I and II, and the wars in Iraq and Afghanistan have impacted manhood in America. Men prefer to isolate themselves, but you cannot have relationships with women or children and remain isolated.

A young man whom I'll call "Will" came into our community program. He had watched his father overdose on drugs. He had no father and his mother rejected him, his brother was aggressive and they had a lot of physical fights. Will developed a lot of hatred and anger. He could not do well in classes and didn't keep up with his work, so he created diversions by being a clown to pull away from his deficiencies. We brought other young men and mentors around Will who were a good example. They became like his family. Later on, Will expressed a desire to get married. He knew he had to do more to be successful in his own life before he could be a husband. He had a transformation based on the positive people who came into his life.

SPENCER

I carry my sh— with me every day. Every day I'm trying to be better. I don't want to live like a politician, where I have to constantly defend myself from my secrets and shameful things I did. I don't want anything to come back on me later. I'm flawed. I'm not proud of it, but I own it.

PART II:
WE'RE NOT THE
HUXTABLES

CHAPTER 3

I CAN'T MAKE YOU LOVE ME

On Saturday night, seven of the fellas joined DJ in his Suburban and traveled an hour for a boxing match, while the others stay back with their significant others and families. On the way back, DJ calls Lamar and Derek on the Bluetooth to fill them in on the fight. Out of the blue, Derek asks Spencer—the only one in the crew without a significant other—why he's not currently dating.

Creep Before You Walk?

SPENCER

The things I lack are what I try to find in other people when I am dating. Most women I dated were victims of child abuse, which affects every part of who you are. I wasn't prepared to deal with those women's issues. They need lifelong therapy. So I put things together as best I could, but I was ill-equipped in my relationship.

I was with a woman who had been molested. Molestation makes you depressed, have low self-esteem and have trust issues with men, so I need to know if you've been through that. A man's joy is to make his woman happy. But if you're dealing with that, I can't make you happy.

> A man's joy is to make his woman happy.

(Looking around the car at his friends)

The only way you can make a relationship work is to truly work on it and know what you're working with. Don't make her feel bad for it when she says you remind her of her stepfather that abused her.

The year before my divorce, I moved into my dad's house, depressed. I learned that being present or giving material things is not the answer—the sadness is still going to be there. Now my attitude is, don't drag me into it, but I'll be here when you come out of it.

JOHN

College was around the time when I started going through bullsh— like sneaking around and being dishonest. I found that I always got the raw end of the deal. I used to compare subsequent dates to my first love, and they were like apples and oranges. You make all these concessions, then you look up and ask, "Where did my life go?"

I should never know that a woman was with five different guys in the same room, but guys talk.

I dated a doctor and a model. I told one, "You've got four guys calling you, and for each one, you acting like he's just your homeboy, and when we're together you talk like I'm just your homeboy." I knew what was up.

JOE

I know a very successful, happily married man with successful, intelligent adult kids. He has a woman on the side in various cities that he sees on his business trips. His attitude is, "I love my wife, but I love her (and her and her) too."

Then there's the machismo factor—"Ah you soft because you love your wife." In the Navy it's custom. In Singapore we was doin' our thing. Some said "I love my wife, I don't wanna catch nothin'." They was on a different level but we tryin' to pressure them to cheat.

DJ

(Points at Joe)

That's what sets people on different levels is if you can be faithful to your wife and support her. It sets you apart.

SPENCER

The thought of being with just one woman is terrifying to men. I gotta put all my eggs in one basket—but I don't want to be hurt again. We are just as emotional as women, even if we don't show it.

I was 23 when I realized I didn't want to have multiple women. The men who do it only do so because they feel the pressure from other men. We really only want one woman. When I am out with my woman, I

We really only want one woman.

get attention from other women. So it's like you're telling me it's okay to sleep with another woman's husband. You can find good men who will help fix a tire, and stay late at work to help out. So why do you want me?

JOHN

This married woman came on to me; she didn't care that either of us were married. She gave me her number, but I didn't call her. Maybe if she looked like Halle Berry, but I still doubt it. I'm not jeopardizing my marriage—it's not worth it, going to counseling and all that. I want my kids to live in a healthy, positive environment.

SPENCER

I cheated for the duration of my marriage. I separated what I did to my wife from who I was. No one has demanded me to be a committed, loyal partner. They accepted my cheating as "just a man being a man." You cannot expect me to be upright and faithful just because I get married—you let me get away with stuff all the time. So I resented black women for allowing us to get away with things. My friend once told me, "If I didn't cheat, do you know how many single women there would be?" Men take advantage of the situation.

DEREK

Before you unzip your pants, you have to think. I bet it never crossed Steve Nair's mind that he would leave his wife and kids on this earth behind some tail.

LAMAR

I think men cheat because they're not getting what they need from their relationship, so they will find it somewhere else, whether it's sex, conversation, or something else.

At one point, everything was dead with Jennifer—I didn't even want to be at home with her. It was like "Hi" and "Bye" and the sex wasn't good anymore. It had been a year, and I wasn't happy. I didn't intend to cheat on my girlfriend. One day while working at a promotional event for my employer, I was approached by someone while I was setting up the booth. She started talking to me and then her sister, Jalisa, came over and started talking to me and continued checking me out during the event. Later that evening, Jalisa grabbed me by the hand and invited me out that night. We sat in a car outside her house and talked all night long. I told her about Jennifer and my situation. Afterward, Jalisa told me she didn't want to deal with me because I had been with Jennifer for so long. She assumed I was married to her. I didn't think she was going to call me, but the next day she did, and it went from there. We now live together and have a 6-year-old son.

So in a way, I didn't really leave Jennifer. We made a mutual decision to go our separate ways. We was just in it to be in it at that point, and we knew it wasn't good for our girls. We have a good friendship now, and we talk every day about all kinds of things—our girls, advice, whatever. Jalisa doesn't like this, but she deals with it because of our kids.

PETE

I struggle with my own conscience. I've been unfaithful a few times. It's been so hard because it's so easy to do. I even get come-ons in the grocery store.

Take this scenario: Your wife has an attractive friend, and you had a thought about gettin' with her. She'd come around even when she knew your wife was not home yet. And perhaps you was giving off a signal of being interested. We're wired to be visual.

Even my in-laws have tried it during trips or when me and my ex-wife[16] lived with them. Like one time when my sister-in-law and I got drunk and had sex. Or when my mother-in-law, who's only 14 years older than my ex-wife, would habitually pop in the bathroom when I wasn't dressed. It happened at least six times. She was prejudiced at first,[17] but then she became curious. After two years of us all living together, I discussed this with my ex-wife and we didn't argue about it. We decided to move out.

The Power of the Tongue

QUINCY

Have you ever had a fight and then later thought, *It wasn't even worth it?* But some people sit on the sidelines enjoying it, even encouraging it, while you're torn up. We get into these piss wars and forget what's important.

I wish we could just stop long enough to say, "What are we fighting for?" You gotta play to win—you don't play to not lose. There's a difference between the two. When you are always in defensive mode, you can't move forward.

---

[16] They were married at the time.
[17] Pete is black; his ex-wife's family is Mexican.

TERRENCE

Women have used my past against me and said things like, "You're never gonna get ahead... you're never gonna change."

QUINCY

Things like that make me feel a resistance. It makes me wonder why should I take her seriously and listen to her if she won't stand by me after the fact. For example: suppose your child begs you for something. When you give it to them, they decide they don't want it, or they don't use it. Now you feel like ignoring them and you don't want to go out of your way for them anymore.

SPENCER

Some black women are hard, independent and opinionated. Women are incredibly defensive. We have to be honest with ourselves before we can have open communication. Lack of proper communication is the main problem. We see communication is key, but communicating what? As men we need to say, "I have problems with my security. I am not as confident as a man as you may think I am." Women assume we are stronger than we really are. They need to know who their man is and what he needs. We all want that one woman where we don't have to go out (looking for someone else).

> **We have to be honest with ourselves before we can have open communication.**

> **Women assume we are stronger than we really are.**

LUIS

Women can accept problems in themselves, but can't tolerate them in other people. If you point out one of their flaws, it's self-deception to them. They'd rather hit that wall of truth than allow you to point it out to them.

QUINCY

I call it the "Eve Effect"[18] when a woman wants to be considered and have a say to influence a decision, but she doesn't want to take any responsibility for the outcome.

SPENCER

I remember one woman I dated—I asked her a lot of questions. She said I was exhausting because I probed so much. She said, "If I had to think back to everything I've been through, I'd go crazy." My response was, "If that would make you crazy, what are you doing now?" We broke up and she hates my guts. It's because I made her have to look at herself.

TERRENCE

Women are good at arguing using hard words, and there's nothing left for us to do but act out. An argument is unstructured and it interferes with the long term goal to live with a woman forever. If she wins the argument, what else can I do? So I'd do something physical to hurt her without touching her. I'd spend everything I had after the bills were paid. I loved sneakers as a kid, but I couldn't have them. Now I own 150 pairs of sneakers. And I've got a nice car, too.

RICO

Some people think arguing is love. They think, *He must care about her because she's staying here.* After an argument, women don't ever forget and keep bringing it up. She keeps throwing it in my face, but I don't—let's move on.

---

[18] Quincy is referring to the Bible story in Genesis 3 about Adam and Eve, in which Eve eats an apple forbidden by God and offers it to Adam, who also eats it.

MICHAEL

Black women are like, "You ain't my daddy," actin' like Ms. Independent. They don't know how to let stuff go.

♟ Fighting Fairly ♟

Melisa Alaba: Poor communication skills cause a lot of anger between men and women. The mistake we make is when we don't understand something the other person has said, and then try to evaluate it and come up with our own conclusions— that may not be true—based on our own experience or limited knowledge. We misinterpret things because we try to get into that other person's head and add emotion to it. So you hear what you think the other person said, but not what they actually said.

One person could also have a lack of insight and mindfulness of himself or herself. Labeling the actions of others and labeling a person are two different things. I don't call you by your mistake, I call you by your name. I had a couple come in for counseling, and the wife repeatedly called her husband "a f—ing liar" during the session. Calling someone a "cheater" or "liar" all the time is not helpful. Sometimes one person in the relationship is truly sorry, their behavior is not habitual, and they are taking steps to get on the right track, but the other person hasn't gotten rid of the fact that the person has changed. They have not let go of the offense, and are still holding onto pain after the situation is over.

Overall, a big reason for dissension and mistrust between black men and women in relationships is that at least one person doesn't want to take responsibility for the relationship. When one person will not to go to counseling at the request of their significant other, their attitude is, "That's your problem— you go," or "That's on you. I said I was sorry." The person that refuses to go to counseling when their partner asks is not committed to maintaining or saving the relationship, and he or she is not willing to make any changes.

Dr. Page: Couples must learn to fight fairly. Temper what you say and do. Watch what you say to each other when you're arguing, understanding that you want the relationship to be there tomorrow. You can't cuss each other out and talk about each other's mothers just because you're mad. You don't have to do that kind of damage just to get your point across. Cussing at someone takes things to another, more demeaning level.

There is no winning and losing. Ask yourself, "What is the issue?" Don't bring up something from a month ago. If the issue is that you want me to help you in the kitchen at night, ask me for help. Make it clear and explain that you won't have energy to have sex if I can't help you in the evening with the kids.

Ask your partner, "What are we gonna do about the problem?" If the solution doesn't work, we need to revisit it. Call him out on it: "You said you would..." and then he has to own up and do it. If he doesn't, he is not interested in solving the problem. But if you care about your relationship, you will work toward that solution.

QUINCY

Why would I want to invest in a stock that pays me no dividends—or that depreciates in value? If she's constantly belittling me with, "You never..." or "Why do you always...," then where does that leave me? Using the words *always* and *never* leaves no room for anything because it's an absolute. It negates or disregards anything I've done right and any efforts I've made on her behalf. My question is: If your man was everything you said he is, what kind of man would he be?

DEREK

You allow people to talk to you the way you do. You fix it by being self-aware. If I'm down and I can look at the woman I chose of my own free will, I can say, "This communication style is not gonna work." Once you can stand up and say that, you can move forward.

TERRENCE

We need to stop tearing each other down. My wife would tear me down. Check yourself—you could deflate someone's goal.

DEREK

Some women don't understand roles. It depends on what their mother instilled in them. I wish there were some old school mamas to teach women, "This is how you talk to a man... Don't do that, boo. Come here, baby, don't do that." Either they're tired or dead and gone. Men are looking for a cheerleader. Be your man's number one supporter and cheerleader. Encourage us. We are very simple! We don't need much. Just be on our side.

PETE

The pen is mightier than the sword, but the tongue ruleth all. What comes out of your mouth comes from your spirit, and that's biblical.[19] When a woman has a mean spirit, it's so close to the devil's work that you don't want to deal with that. You want to have a clean spirit unless you're trying to protect your kids or something, but you shouldn't make yourself feel better than someone else by belittling them.

DEREK

(Shifts in his seat and waves his hands intently as he talks)

When you're married, your wife puts up a mirror to you and says, "This is you." The two becoming one flesh[20] is a lifelong process, so you have to have a grace-based marriage. Let the

---

[19] Pete is referring to a Bible reference: Matthew 12:34b.
[20] This phrase is a Bible reference to Genesis 2:22–24.

other person go through their thing because we're all human. We have to get down the road and say, "Forgive me, babe, I messed up. My bad. I'm sorry. You were right." Pride and insecurity keep us from saying these things. You have to be man enough to apologize—you're not right all the time. Don't get stuck on that point. Keep it moving. Otherwise, resentment, bitterness, anger and hatred will come in, and now I'm in competition with my spouse. The attitude is like, "I got one up on you and I'll get you back." It's childish.

TERRENCE

Men need to get better at loving their women. If a woman lashes out on you, don't assume that she has no respect for you, but understand that there may be something else going on, or a roadblock in that area. Ask her what's wrong and try to help her through it. It's my responsibility to communicate where I think a lack of respect lies and what respect means to me. Have some consideration for what she needs, which is love, and where the breakdown is. Like if she's not feeling the love she needs, or if I need more respect.

> It's my responsibility to communicate where I think a lack of respect lies and what respect means to me.

SPENCER

> If you know how to nurture your woman, she will submit and be the woman you want her to be—and not have to be co-captain.

JOHN

We're not taught or groomed on how to choose mates. We say things like, "She got a nice shape, she's cute," or "Make sure he's got a job."

I was so in love with a woman, I overlooked everything. You go through it because she's fine, or you thought you had something in common. One of you may say something, and you think *Wow, this guy gets me!* or *I gotta be with her*, but it's physical chemistry.

You want to be with someone, be touched, have a friendship—it's normal. But we pick the wrong partners. What do they believe in? Do they have any books? Do they read? Do they pay attention to the news? If she was my soul mate, she would've been with me for the rest of my life. We choose folks who might be good for someone else, but not us.

You want somebody that fits with you. A four-part piece might fit in a five-part piece, but something is still missing.

TONY

I don't want a woman like my mom; I want someone better than her. She has to drop her guard and open her heart and mind so she knows I'm with her even when I'm many miles away. Insecurity can come from magazines, TV, and other influences. I love a thick woman.

I was with my wife for four years before we got married. You get a reward off of having a family. I'd love to be married again. I wanna get married; I want a woman to captivate and motivate me—someone who grasps me from a distance. Even though I'm not present with you every day, I'm with you every day.

SPENCER

We're not being taught as men how to start a relationship with a woman and keep it intact.

DEREK

Each woman has to decide and know within herself whether she is the one for the man she thinks she wants. It's part of your faith walk. Ask God, "Is this the one You want me to be with?" Get serious. Be honest and real with yourself.

As a leader and man, you have to understand the nature of humans and the dynamics between man and woman. Women want to be covered, protected, and girded regardless of who makes more money. Any time those roles are reversed, there's going to be chaos. You have to get instructions on how to lead from God. He talks to leaders differently than he talks to followers.

I wanted to find a wife based on finding someone compatible with my life purpose. I can tell who a man is by the woman he chooses, and whether a man knows who he is by the woman he chooses. Once you know who you are, you will choose a woman that fits that purpose.

♟ Choosing the Ideal Mate ♟

Melisa Alaba: People need to have expectations of a potential relationship. You should have some idea of what your relationship is going to look like, or what you want it to look like from the start so you can wind up with one that is healthy. What do you want? How do you want to be treated? What does good communication look like to you? How do you argue fairly? People want to be able to talk to their partners. Some men in the conversation discussed women's emphasis on evaluating their job or money situation, but those things are important, as well as the compatibility of your mindset and goals. If you're ambitious and the other person is not, it's gonna be an issue. You do not necessarily have to make six figures, but be on same page. If one person is a go-getter and the other person spends it all, you won't make progress as a couple.

Dr. Page: When you're thinking about dating, some things that both men and women should do are: self-reflect, understand who you are, have good self-esteem, have a job, and get your goals together. Make sure you do all these things before you even approach someone. Don't say you have no role model for how to do it right—if you have to, you can look at President Obama, who loves his wife and family.

Women who find a man who is clueless should *RUN!* You can't change a man. The way he is is the way he will stay. No amount of love, uniqueness, or sex will change things. Have standards that you will not negotiate. Ask each other questions, like where you see yourself in five years. Don't just let it flow "to see where things go"—there's too much at risk.

Dr. Utley: I believe in civil unions for everyone. People divorce because they don't talk about money, sex, children, or future goals from the beginning. I think people should be forced to put all of those core issues down on paper and sign a contract that declares what happens if they change their minds. Love is awesome, but it's not enough to put a forever on. People should also seek pre-marital counseling and spend at least four seasons with each other so they know after one year how people adjust to the various times of the year.

People should look for a partner in a mate. Not someone who will make you whole. You should be whole all by yourself. Two whole people can better articulate their insecurities and their issues. People should marry because they want to partner with someone—work together as a team, be a true "us"—not just "it's you or me," but sometimes we come together.

Healthy relationships need models. Find couples who you admire and spend time with them. Of course, no one is perfect, but people who have weathered storms you are about to face are a wealth of information.

Society supports the idea that sex is a man's conquest. Pick a movie: Guy chases the girl until they have sex. Men feed women and take them on dates to ensure sex. Women are taught that their power rests in the ability to control men's access to sex, and while the game looks fun on the screen, many men begin to resent women who they feel are controlling their desires. This resentment turns to misogyny and more violent encounters with women whether they be imagined or in real life.

Dr. Page: Another thing you should do is be active in your children's dating life. I take my daughters (ages 17 and 14) out on dates. We had a talk about five types of boys they will come across:

> **Be active in your children's dating life.**

- The Momma's Boy: If his mother does not select someone as her potential daughter-in-law, she will never be good enough for her son. The woman will always struggle to be accepted by this mother. Never being able to fit in with his mother, she will become frustrated and disappointed with the development of the relationship. He will never break the emotional bond with his mother even if the woman does everything right. In her eyes, she (the girlfriend) will never do things right—like she (the mother) does.

- The Bad Boy: This is a guy who always seems to get in trouble, but it is never his fault. Life has dealt him a bad hand. He complains that he has had a hard life. Growing up in a single parent household, his father left the family while he was very young. He tells the woman that she has the best life, with a father and a mother who support and love her. If only he had this support and love, he would have been a better person. The bad boy will play on her emotions and her desire to help him turn his life around. While she is trying to help him, she is consistently imitating his bad habits and delaying her plans for success because she does not want him to feel left behind.

- The Pretty Boy: This guy is charming, has dazzling looks and a smile that will warm your heart on the coldest of days. The pretty boy is hard to say no to and resist. Because he is attractive, he is often bombarded by girls and has a difficult time saying no to their advances. The pretty boy will judge a woman and decide whether it is appropriate for her to be with him. If she is not attractive or popular, she considers it a blessing that he gives her any attention.

- The Athletic Boy: Women are attracted to him, whether handsome, average-looking or not at all attractive, simply because of his physical talents and abilities. School officials, his parents, and other girls will often give him accolades because he is involved in sports and successful at them. The greater his talents and abilities are, the more popular he will be. He is also bombarded by girls and has a hard time saying no to their advances.

- The Smooth Boy: He may or may not be the most attractive, but he possesses the gift of a being able to "smooth talk" his way out of any situation. Convincing and deceiving, he tells lies and makes them sound like the truth. Along with being a smooth talker, he has the ability to make a woman laugh and feel special. He is very easy to talk to and dresses in an appealing way.

Once I explained these five types of boys, I showed my daughters how to deal with each one. They came back later and told me about boys they met later, and they were able to recognize and identify their types: "Daddy, he was a pretty boy; he tried to be smooth..."

I remember one time with my 17-year-old (who was 16 at the time) where I ate lunch with a boy that liked her at school. I would let her date once a month (those were the ground rules that I set), but I had to meet the boy first—then I'd allow them to go to the movies. I wouldn't drop her off at the food court at the mall and leave like she and her mother insisted I do. I put my foot down and explained that I needed to go into the mall with her for safety reasons. Good thing I did, because one time the boy who was supposed to meet up with her was late. I stayed with her to meet the boy, then left. I picked her up at the food court at the end of the date.

My daughter thought this whole thing was lame, but I had to sit down and talk to her and explain why I was going through all these steps with her instead of dropping her off or being nonchalant about her dating. I told her, "I'm scared because I'm losing my baby. I'm not just being paranoid or overprotective." I had to show her my emotional side, and that was something that resonated with her. I talk to her about limits she should set whether she's at home or not. I can't be with her all the time so I want her to be able to set her own personal boundaries.

DJ

The number one mistake women make is, they get married so they won't be bouncin' from man to man... but are they ready? A girl I know—one of her best friends got married to someone she met on the internet after six months. The man is a father, paying child support to two different women. She didn't court him, rushed everything, and her life turned upside down (she didn't want his kids moving in with them).

DEREK

As a man, you look at yourself setting the pace for a relationship, according to what society says. What do I need to find in the mate that will walk beside me?

I had to tell myself: What do all my relationships have in common? I had sex with these women before I knew who they were. I'm gonna do something radically different. I'm gonna keep my clothes on. The next woman I met was my wife. So I decided that for once, I really want to get to know who this person is. Sex is something that's always gonna be there. You spend less than 20 percent of your life in bed having sex. We made that commitment together. Our whole year of courtship, through medical issues, credit issues, and the kids—I had to know I liked this person! When you're not wearing the rose-colored glasses of hips, lips, and fingertips, you can make sober-minded decisions. Yeah, you fine, you cute, but what else are you? Are we going in the same direction? On our second date I spilled my guts—because I knew she was "The One." And she came back. No games.

> What do all my relationships have in common? I had sex with these women before I knew who they were.

At certain ages and stages as a man, you should have something to put your piece on the board of life to be in a relationship. You gotta have money, home, car as an entrance point. Know who you are and where you're going. Have direction. Have a place that you can call home to bring someone into. You are the king of your own castle. That other stuff will come. Operate from a place of strength and not weakness. There's nothing you can tell a man who has a place of his own. But you can also be stuck to the place you are where you're not willing to change.

If you don't know better, you won't do better. Get with a men's ministry. We gotta do better about talking to these young men. Don't disrespect them, just be cool and let them holla at you. Let them know how to act and how to treat a lady. Don't come at 'em trippin'. You

> You always have to be progressive and moving forward. Men stop growing; women catch up and then pass them.

always have to be pro-gressive and moving forward. Men stop growing; women catch up and then pass them.

(Lamar nods.)

Bad Karma

JOE

If I met the one I wanna be with, can I trust her, after all I've done? You reap what you sow—it's karma. I got plans to meet a married woman on Friday—she called me—and I know this woman is well taken care of and her husband treats her well... I don't know who I can trust.

(Sighs)

We are hesitant to be 100 percent[21] because of what *we're* doing.

RICO

Yeah... we know we're doing wrong.

(Takes a sip of his beer)

QUINCY

Society says, "Trust no one." So as long as I can't count on you or open up to you, that won't happen. It's all predicated whether **It's impossible for me to heal or to bond with you if I feel you're a threat.** I believe you won't hurt me, cheat on me, or go and do something behind my back. It's impossible for me to heal or to bond with you if I feel you're a threat.

---

[21] Faithful.

PETE

I don't want to have to work for a relationship. I don't have faith in relationships. There's a lot of self-doubt in general, too... I didn't think I was deserving or worthy of a strong, viable, rewarding, fruitful relationship. Maybe that's because of my parents' relationship. I'm not confident it can happen.

The Goodies

After some of the fellas go to church and then to brunch with their families on Sunday morning, they meet in the afternoon at the neighborhood community center to swim or lift weights. In the sauna, they talk about one of their favorite subjects (sex) and their not-so-favorite subject (marriage).

RICO

If we stop having sex with a woman, it's because we're turned off by her attitude. When you hear, "Nigga I don't need you, I'mma leave," my attitude is, "Well then, leave."

DEREK

Women need to be careful what they tell the opposite sex about their marriage. They try to compare two totally different situations, and that's where they get in trouble.

QUINCY

Women want us to talk about our feelings, but women don't want to hear the truth. I could start off **Women don't want to hear the truth.** with something like, "I'm having a hard time with this because I feel like you're not showing me enough affection." But then it all goes to hell.

If a woman feels like her husband's interest is waning, she should approach him from the standpoint of "What is it that he's missing?" Not, "Oh I'mma show him!" A lot of times people are quick to tell you what they're *not* gonna do in a relationship *way* more than what they're willing to do: *(moving his neck in jest)* "I ain't doin' all that! If he need that he need to find somebody else 'cause I ain't the one." Then when he does...

RICO

Right! If other women are showing me attention and affection, but you only want to have sex twice a month? Are you serious?

When we're in a relationship with you, we want to get along with you. We fall in love, too. But withholding sex as punishment is not a good idea. We are protective. Our ego says, "If she's not giving me sex, she's giving it to someone else." We think like that. Take care of us—I'm too tired to go find someone else and run the streets—makes me think of the song "Every Dog Needs a Home."[22] Remember Bernie Mac said, "30 pumps and we done." Once we bust one, we're goin' to sleep. We do all that other stuff for y'all! You might be tired, but we only need three minutes!

(Laughter)

TONY

Sometimes women are manipulative. What I learned in sales about selling to women is that they always go with the glamour, city boy, flashy, clean-cut stuff. They want to have a conversation but can't have one without it leading to sex.

Drugs and alcohol are triggers commonly used to lead to sex and they create faulty ideas of what's there when it's not really there. Some of the younger ones stay in that cloudiness of mind and they can't get past these extras.

---

[22] A song by DMX and Aaliyah.

PETE

Talking to women should be like simple like 1+1 but now it's some complicated equation like 4^2. I like "cerebral combat": we can just debate about something—I ain't tryin' to be right, I just want to understand the concept. Stretch my mind, then we can stretch guts.

JOE

I'm not good at detecting when a woman likes me. On another note, if I really like a woman who is celibate, even if she's the right one, I can't wait around for six months, so I'll probably have something on the side.

Take This Ring Off

LUIS

When we get to about 32, 34, we think, *I need to be married; I don't wanna be with that many more women.*

(Michael nods excitedly and laughs.)

So the next one is the best one and we make her The One.

MICHAEL

(Pointing at Luis)

The next one who is pretty and can cook.

LUIS

(Laughing)

Hah! It don't even take all that!

(Bumps fists with Michael)

DJ

I was married for 15 years and I've been divorced two years. I got married when I had my third child.

Being married is good for a man. I got married young and stayed in the marriage for the kids. I learned a whole lot. If I get into a new marriage I know what I'm looking for because I know myself better now. It's all a learning experience—every day when you wake up. What I learned: I am definitely marriage material. I realize the mistake I made the first time is that I got married for the wrong reason, because I had kids. I wanted to be in my sons' lives.

God instituted marriage for love—it's for people who are mentally ready and open to it. Some women are not ready and don't know how to be wives. A lot of times they marry for the wrong reasons but are tryin' to do the right thing. Support your husband and be a wife, but be honest with yourself—don't be a follower. I'm finna be raisin' your kids. Consider counseling and be open for a blended family. You saying your child can't come live with us? Nah, that's not the right attitude—so they're not mentally ready.

RICO

I've been with my wife for over 20 years. We have a 6-year-old son and twin 18-year-old daughters. I filed for divorce—I feel like I'm divorced because we've been separated for four years. I'm going on with my life, but she's holding things up. Dudes ask me: "20 years? How'd you last that long?" Marriage is supposed to be forever—even five years is an accomplishment. Marriage is not a bad thing, but it's met with negativity. You gotta work for it.

SPENCER

Man, I knew my marriage was wrong three months in. I got married out of obligation because we dated for five years. I knew how to stay married, but not how to keep the marriage fresh and alive. There was no romance—just a familiar connection who was "safe" to be with.

JOE

You gotta be on the same page. Both of you have to be committed. I'm a serial dater but I don't want to keep doing it until I'm 50, especially since I have a daughter. I guarantee you that if Sarah brought dudes around my daughter, I'd have a fit. I can't play with my ex-girlfriends' kids.

Sarah tried to get back with me for a couple of years... she'd mention it in conversation or come to the door naked when I came to pick up our daughter (as a baby). It's not right to do it but as a man it's hard resist sometimes. I sometimes thought that I might as well stay with her, but no, I wasn't happy. We get along now.

LAMAR

You know what? I don't want to get married. It's not for me, and I have two reasons:

(Holds out his hand and sticks one finger out, counting)

Number 1: My mother was not married to my father; he's been married to someone else since before I was born. His wife knew about his other relationships and his kids born from those relationships. So by my mother not ever having been married, it makes me not want to get married.

(Counts on the second finger of the same hand)

Number 2: I'm very picky. If I'm in a relationship and I'm not getting something that I think a marriage should have, I back away and keep my guard up.

(Tommy nods.)

For example, I like a clean house and I like stuff to be organized. If I see something out of the ordinary, I'm not thinking about getting married, because I know it's not gonna change the way that person is. Being in a long relationship and living together is just like being married anyway.

My ex didn't ask us to get married, but she mentioned it and at one point I did consider it. My girlfriend now? She mentions it on a consistent basis. She says she doesn't see herself being with someone for a long time and not be married to him. We discussed this in the beginning and I was up front with her on my views about marriage, but now she's trying to change my mind.

I will say this in spite of everything: if I ever got into a relationship where the woman holds me down in every way possible, I could change my mind about getting married!

TOMMY

(Shakes his head)

I don't have any feeling that I have to be in a relationship—I can be everything I want and can get it on my own. A lot of guys are in relationships for financial reasons, motherly nurturing—but I'm not like that. I once told my son's mother in court that I don't need a woman but for one thing.

(Laughter)

I've always said that I'm not gonna get married. To me, loneliness is only a phone call away.[23] That's why I'm always so busy. I don't strive to have a family... I wasn't raised with that mindset, so it's not something I strive for. I strive for contentment in myself. A majority of men I know—family, friends, associates, acquaintances—they always tell me "Don't do it" when it comes to marriage, including my father. They say, "Take your time to find exactly what you want." The men I know go out and get married, they're unhappy, and they play the role. But once they get some freedom, they go buck wild. I think their mindset is, "I don't know

---

[23] Meaning, you don't have to be lonely because you can always call someone.

when is the next time I'll get to go out, so I'll go wall to wall." Some guys aren't like that, but a majority are.

I know this guy who's been with this girl less than a year and is getting her a ring, but they argue a lot. Why would you put yourself in that situation? I won't put up with something I don't like—I don't have to deal with it. But these guys settle. I've just never been the type of person to settle. Certain things about the mindset of the person they settle for are just not right. The women may have a desire to change something about the dude. People know what they're getting into before marriage, but they don't look at the signs; then later on down the line they act like they never saw that[24] before. But you saw the signs.

(Several of the men nod.)

It's like the job interview process—you're the best person you can be in the interview—you're not being exactly how you really are. But with time you get to see all the problems you don't want to deal with. These guys do things prematurely. It's hard for them to say they want to take a break and analyze the situation because they don't want to give up their comfort zone, even if there's heartache involved.

I'm picky. I remember one time a girl said I had commitment issues. It's not that—I just don't want to settle. There's certain things I don't want to tolerate. You might be cool and we may only want to connect physically, but I don't want to feel like I'm using you. It's hard to get in a situation and deal with someone without hurting her feelings. It's all about what you're willing to deal with.

PETE

Look. I wanted to get married one time.

(Holds out one finger for emphasis)

---

[24] Bad behavior.

My ex-wife was the person I have loved the most in all my life. I don't think I could love anyone with that threshold again. If I could take back 15 years of crap, I would still be with her. She knows me and she gave me the opportunity to come back at one point. You do some things in marriage early on you that you don't do after you've had three kids. By not taking that opportunity, I may have taken a chunk out of her spirit. I said no because I was thinking I could get something else—at that time I had access to a lot of enhancing stimulus. There's a thrill to being a player that you didn't get being monogamous, along with my little business making $10,000 a pop and parlaying that into other things, kinda like an Eazy-Z or Tony Montana mentality.

DEREK

The Bible says you're supposed to cleave to your spouse, but we make up our own rules. It's a simple concept but if you don't follow it, you ain't ready for marriage. You wonder why your spouse won't talk to you when you're not being open-minded? Your spouse should come first, but we got all these selfish motives.

QUINCY

Men have a problem when we're told that it's not okay to feel how we feel. You dismiss my feelings when you say, "Oh just get over it." The reason all this matters is because when you want me to take you seriously as my partner, and you want me to give my all, you need to do the same. The way we give and respond to things is different.

TONY

To be with us, women should be optimistic, positive, and open-minded. Weak women don't need to put everything on a platter. There are men out here who are trying to do what's right and put in work. Don't bring no baggage from that man who pissed you off and you wanted to castrate him.

Stimulate, captivate, motivate my mind and sex appeal. Relax and don't be stressful. Stress is the #1 killer of black women.

SPENCER

When I get married again, I know I'm gonna have to be honest and open enough to say who I am and where I come from. I want us to be able to grow together.

Intimacy goes far beyond sex. I need to find a person I can grow with and who is willing to understand me and vice versa. I need to know what her life was like before me, and vice versa.

When you play on a team, you have to know what your teammate is not capable of, or afraid of. If a woman is trying to audition for a role in my life and hiding who she really is, we both wake up with each other a few years later wondering who the hell we're next to. No one has really changed. We're just afraid to show each other who we are in the beginning.

We're just afraid to show each other who we are in the beginning.

I had to let go of the fallacy that things are going to stay peachy all the time. They're not. The truth is, I didn't know what I wanted or needed. The kind of relationship I want is one that I've never seen. Went through so much that I thought I could fix it. I was just trying to be the answer to the problem.

TERRENCE

If I look back on my life, I can see how I used to think and what I used to do. I'm open-minded now. I used to date with a guarded heart but now I will date you and hand my heart to you. And if you can't protect it, I'll take it back. That scares people.

I'm at the point in my life now where if God blesses me and gives me the chance to get married again, I think I know what to do now.

(Derek gives Terrence a pat on the back, then heads to the locker room. The others follow suit.)

CHAPTER 4

THE PRICE ISN'T RIGHT

Joe invited everyone to a card party at his house on Sunday night. The women decide to stay upstairs to eat and chitchat in front of the TV while the fellas head to the basement. Quincy gets a phone call from his daughter's mother[25] and steps outside.

Cory, Tony, Terrence and DJ are playing spades. The others are sitting or standing nearby with their beers or phones in hand. Quincy comes in the room 30 minutes later, visibly agitated.

The Blame Game

QUINCY

(Exasperated)

When it comes to baby mama drama, no matter what the father is doing for their child, the man is required to be the villain. Someone has to be the bad guy, and it's always the man.

DEREK

If anything goes wrong in a relationship, the first person that they turn to is the man.

---

[25] From a previous relationship, not his current wife.

RICO

Yup. The ones who don't do anything... the ones who are bums? They ain't on child support. But when it comes to the men who are responsible, and the ones who already take care of their kids, women put those men on child support because they wanna hurt us because we're not with them anymore.

♟ Someone Has to Step Up ♟

Rachelle Miller: I sit in mediations with parents time and time again, and usually what it comes down to is that someone does not want to cooperate and do their part. The court has to get involved to force someone's hand. Most of the time, one person is just not doing their part and going to court is a last resort. If you do your part on the front end, chances are you won't have to go to court.

There's a perception that when one parent wants the other to pay child support, it's some kind of punishment or a life altering betrayal. Yes, in some cases there could be manipulation going on, but most sane folk don't want to go through the hassle of dealing with an agency, court, or lawyer.

You can make choices to avoid court. You shouldn't have to press the issue on the court, but often, one person is not stepping up and being responsible. Every woman does not want to be vindictive. But if they have no recourse, there's nothing else they can do.

TOMMY

Sometimes the mother is the biggest holdback. I take the blame for some things, but sometimes the father is trying to work with the mother, but if it's not exactly the way she wants things to be, we have lots of arguments.

My work schedule wouldn't allow me to stay on schedule with visitations for my oldest son. Instead of trying to understand about my work schedule, his mother took me to court numerous times. I explained this to the judge, but he still wanted to hold me in violation of my visitation. Due to a breakup or whatever, it takes a while to deal with each other and realize that what you're doing is supposed to be for the child. I've always been involved in my child's life. I couldn't be at every basketball game or coach his team, and sometimes I can't make my visitation arrangements because of work, but when I can, I'm there.

My youngest son's mother threatened to take me to court because she doesn't get child support when she wants it. One time she took pictures with our son, and I said I'd give her money that week, but not the same day she asked for it. She went into an uproar—"You're doing what you wanna do..."—but I was going to pay for the pictures and give her money for child support. She wouldn't work with me. In all actuality, that's what she agreed to (receive money when I get paid on the 1st and 15th of the month).

As far as the guys that are trying to do good, it's not that the guy is not trying to do his part; it's the mother we can't get along with. Sometimes one's attitude or desires play into what they want and not what's best for the child. It takes working together. When it comes to deadbeats (of the women I've dated), the children would be just as excited to see their fathers whether they pay or not. I think it has to do with the attitude of the mother. Some women don't take their exes to court and decide, "I'll do it on my own." Then if the guy is like, "Hey, I wanna see them," she's like, "I'm not letting you." The men that do more for their children seem to get punished... the ones who do the bare minimum, they argue with women, the ones who do nothing—they don't have to do anything. I don't understand why women let those men get away with not paying. If he's living and breathing, he should have to pay child support. *(Rico nods his head forcefully and sighs.)*

Custody shouldn't be about who has a better support system, but who has the better environment? And the child support thing can be unfair for a man. Now get this: my oldest son lived with me for two years previously. When I had custody, he was with me for four months before I stopped paying her child support. I didn't put her on child support because I knew she didn't have much money. I was thinking that the next two years he lives with her, that I won't have to pay it. Nope. She wanted it. She was an alcoholic. Now she's trying to take me to get back child support!

My son's been locked up for the past five months, and he's not getting out until after he turns 18, but last month his mother took me to court again. I think if my son were not in jail I would have had to pay, but the judge said, "He's in the custody of the state," so there's no point. When it comes to my younger son, I don't have any documentation of paying his mother, so they could get me for seven years of not paying.

♟ It's Not About You ♟

Rachelle Miller: Some parents are under the impression that they are in child support court to get their way. Most of the judges in family court are men. Their job is to weigh the evidence and determine the best interest of the child.

Often, new parents are unaware of the expenses that come with raising a child. Men are unprepared when it comes to having children. Getting school clothes for your kid is nice, but they also need housing, food, and healthcare. And those clothes you bought last year will not last long for your growing child. Doctor visits, medications, afterschool care—it's all expensive. You may think your child support contribution is a big thing, but it's not.

The court looks at evidence. Keep a paper trail of payments—even automatic payments from a bank account create a record of payment that is admissible in court. This kind of evidence counters the lies of a manipulative or greedy baby mama.

Some men pay child support to avoid suspension of their driver's license and going to jail, but they don't visit their kids. A client once asked me, "Can I make him visit his children?" No. Their legal duty is to pay. You can't make someone be involved or take their access.

No matter what the case is in court, both parents should nurture their relationships with their children.

Is it Mine?

JOE

When I found out I was gonna be a dad, I was skeptical about if it was mine. You know how many times I've been told that? But once I saw my daughter, I was done. I was at a hospital working and she was at another hospital giving birth—her friend told me Sarah was in labor and I went. I saw how light the baby was, and subconsciously I'm trying to get out of it and thinking, is she mine? But the second time I saw her, I had a flashback to my atrocious picture as a boy and I saw a bit of me, but I still got a blood test. I know some scandalous chicks. One of my boys paid for a little girl for three years that wasn't his.

JOHN

I don't know if anyone plans to have babies these days—not until your 30s and 40s—because by then, time is running out. My wife was 44 when she had our daughter. When a woman gets pregnant and you come back with, "Are you sure it's mine?" that sets off the distrust.

If you're not ready to have kids with a woman, don't sleep with her, or else get a vasectomy because condoms are not 100 percent foolproof. In my early 20s, I was with a West Indian woman whom I had known for four months and I had sex with her three times. One of those times the condom broke and she missed her period. I told her, "We don't really know each other. I don't really love you and you don't really love me." She went off, saying "How you gonna tell me how I feel?" and went into cussing and insults. Turns out she was never pregnant, but she made me sweat it out!

That's What It's Made For

MICHAEL

I wanted to have a mental connection with a woman before a physical one. I spent two and a half years being celibate and was looking for virgins on purpose so there would be no pressure for sex. But by the time I was 22 or 23, I had two kids. Once you get a taste of the nectar, it's hard to not have it anymore.

My oldest two sons are nine months apart. You know Usher's song "That's What It's Made For"? That song describes how my firstborn was created.

I was in college in Mississippi. This girl Carmen was the sister of one of my frat brothers. She liked me, but I respected her so I didn't mess with her. We went to her spot to hang out sometimes but I didn't bring a condom so I wouldn't be tempted. I learned a few things about myself and my confidence started building. The girls used to like when I licked my lips. I had a nice body and I was fit and trim, so I thought I was a rather appealing fella. I was a jackrabbit with like 40, 50 women. Carmen was one of the first women I had unprotected sex with.

On the night in question, during finals week, Carmen kissed me. I told her to stop. She did it again. Then we started making out and it led to intercourse.

I don't remember why I didn't pull out. I thought "F—! She could have a baby; I could have a disease..." But I decided, "F— it" and I kept having sex with her all night. That was a Thursday. On the following Thursday—she called and told me she was pregnant. It had to be a three-way call because Carmen didn't have my number. (She called her girlfriend, who called her boyfriend, and then he called me.)

My first two thoughts? 1) I knew what she was gonna say. 2) This is some bullsh—.

I asked her, "How do you know you're pregnant after seven days?" She said, "I know my body." So did it happen before? I knew she had a reputation, and I felt like I was being set up. I was a young black male on the honor roll. I was gonna be somebody. I wasn't an athlete, I was a "mathlete."

I asked her, "Why would you wanna have a child when we don't hardly know each other, and we're in school? Should we f— up our lives and come to school with a child?" She said, "For once in my life I want to have someone who loves me." I've heard that from *several* women. I asked her to come to L.A. (my hometown) and transfer to school there so we could see if we could be together and make it happen.

She wanted to have a baby so she'd have someone that would love her.

I don't know why, but we stopped talking that summer. When I went back to Mississippi that August, a few days before school started, people who I didn't even know came up to me saying things like, "I heard you got a baby on the way." There were over 15,000 students at this school, so how did they know? Rumors went around that Carmen could be pregnant by this nigga or that nigga, so she could've already been pregnant when I slept with her.

Stupidity kicked in again about four or five months later. I met Maria, and we had unprotected sex over the holidays. She was my girlfriend and I loved her. That's when my second son was conceived. A week later, while Maria's head was in my lap and I was rubbing her pregnant stomach, I got a phone call from Carmen. She told me our son had been born.

During the next semester, five girls approached me back at the dorm. They had a yearbook and pointed to this guy who they said was Carmen's baby daddy. Carmen's brother even came up to me and told me that it was a football player's baby. These were two unrelated events where people are telling me, "That ain't your baby." Sure enough, the baby was light skinned with curly hair like the football player.

Then I got a child support letter, but I was cool. I tried to convince Carmen to take a blood test, but she refused. She told me "Take it upon yourself to pay for day care."

I withdrew from school at that point. Maria was in a different part of the state for law school and I wanted to be with her. Two weeks later Maria gave birth to my second son. We didn't work out, so at the end of following spring semester, I went back home to L.A.

I had my son[26] for about eight months while she did an internship for law school. Then she went home. I sent money, visited on holidays, and all that.

When my firstborn turned 5, Carmen got married. Her husband wanted to adopt my son. I said I wanted a DNA test first, and she did everything she could to block it. I paid for it. Turns out he was mine! He looks like one of my cousins—nothing like me. I signed the adoption papers. She had two more kids with this guy before they married. My lawyer said we needed to add a clause that said she could not keep me from my son, but I'm thinking that she's a woman of her word and would never do that. But she came back with, "For the sake of my child, I don't think you're fit to be a father." So we went to court.

During the court proceedings, I met Kim.

I was on child support once, but only because Maria filed on me while we were living together. It was after we had a fight about having kids because I told her I didn't want to have kids. I didn't want her to keep it and she said "It's my body and I can do what I want

---

[26] His son with Maria.

to." I asked her to sign something saying I wouldn't be responsible for anything having to do with the baby. I was young and dumb and didn't know sh— about the world. I apologized to her later.

I bought school clothes and paid for all my son's travel arrangements, so there was no reason to put me on child support. Then Maria found out that my girlfriend Kim was pregnant. She said, "I'm gonna get you for child support." I said, "You're an attorney. You make way more money than me." She eventually dropped the threats, and I married Kim.

If Maria ever tried to keep our son from me, I would call her mother and she'd be my advocate. It helps being a good guy and knowing you're a good guy.

Seven years ago, I investigated moving to Georgia with my three kids[27] because I wanted to be closer to my two oldest kids. Maria got mad when I told her I was moving closer to Mississippi. I just wanted to get an update on our son. Then three years ago, she told our son that her husband was not his biological father, and he wanted to know about me. He doesn't call me "Dad," he calls me Michael, and that's fine because I didn't raise him. He has a lot of animosity toward me. My oldest two sons became friends on Facebook and began talking about their siblings and family.

♟ Is it Worth It? ♟

Rachelle Miller: I noticed that no one in this conversation[28] wanted to take responsibility for their part with regard to their situation. It's all about the blame game. Some of these guys are just making bad choices and being irresponsible. Someone is not stepping up.

---

[27] With his wife, Kim.
[28] Except Tommy.

> The first thing I'd tell single people is make wise decisions from the start. Evaluate the personality traits of your partner. Avoid the court system altogether if possible. Depending on how crazy your ex is, you could be in and out of court for awhile. Is a quick lay worth it?

A Motherless Child

JOHN

My daughter's mother Larissa and I never got along because we had a big age difference. We were seven years apart and we didn't have the same things in common. When you're younger, age matters!

I was 30 when I had my first daughter. Larissa always threatened to take her away. She called the cops whenever I yelled back—no one ever did that to me before.

After a big fight we broke up and she took 15 percent of my gross income. I walked 80 blocks from 56th Street and 11th Avenue in Manhattan—that's how depressed I was. Our baby was almost three then, so at least she knew me. I had our daughter a few days a week. I watched the baby while I was in night school. It was the worst three years of my life—the stone ages.

Eventually Larissa told me she wanted to have fun with her life, and wanted to give all parental rights to me. She'd say things like, "I'm too young for all this sh—," or "You'll see when I don't come to pick her up tonight."

A month later, she got pregnant and wanted us to celebrate (the baby's father had a wife who was also pregnant). She said, "She can stay with me while you get settled," but I knew it would be awhile. Larissa only wanted custody so she could keep getting child support. And she wanted to increase it even though I had no increase in pay and had our daughter half the month. So she would come at me with stuff like, "You gonna have to pay me my money."

Clothes and other expenses should come out of child support. So I sent her my paystub and a total breakdown of my bills and expenses. But she'd be like, "I don't give a f— how you get the money—ask your mother, ask your girlfriend, collect cans or sell drugs, motherf—er! I want my money." She tried to penalize me, even though I was doing more than I was supposed to.

I told her boyfriend what was going on. He said, "Don't worry, I got you." Ten minutes later she called and said "Forget it—don't worry about it." I just wanted peace—it was so toxic dealing with her.

(As he finishes this story, his wife comes downstairs and asks him to help her with something upstairs.)

The Papers

TONY

Four years ago, I got child support papers notifying me that I supposedly had a 5-year-old child. I didn't know anything about it. The baby mama lives 20 minutes from my grandma and could have gotten in contact with me, even though she said she couldn't find me. She doesn't want to do a DNA test and won't let me see my daughter.

CORY

(Turns to Tony, signaling that it's his turn)

When my son's mother went on welfare, the state forced her to apply for child support to repay the state for the benefits she was receiving. That was a rude awakening. The child support process showed me blatantly how men don't get a fair shot. I saved two shoeboxes full of receipts for things spent on my son, and I told the judge, "I'm already paying for my son, so why do I have to go on child support?"

TONY

(Eyes bulging, he slaps his leg)

Exactly!

CORY

I felt like she could have got a job, but since she was on government assistance, I had to pay child support. The judge said, "Son, this is the land of the law and I'm just here to execute it."

(Tony shakes his head.)

MICHAEL

My father still owes about $40,000 of child support for me to this day! I spent so much time with him though. Why is that bill there? I never asked my parents why, but maybe I should.

JOE

I tried to work it out with Sarah, and just paid for day care at first. Then we had argument about what I was paying at that time, and didn't want to pay more. I can see when your child is 1 to 5 because of how expensive day care is, but with an older child it's a little different because you will need to live somewhere whether you have a child or not. Do school clothes and food really cost that much? $700?

(Rico gives him an exaggerated stare and Quincy shakes his head.)

But I'll take care of my kid. I don't go to court to try to reduce it. I'll be there for my daughter. I just don't like if she's wearing shoes with holes in them, but other than that I'm good. I just want the most for her as possible.

CORY

The court system is not designed to care about you or your family. If I had been weaker I wouldn't have wanted anything to do with my son after that court business. They look at a formula, like 70/30. I had to pay 70 percent! Courts don't get mothers to do things.

♟ Bias in the Court ♟

Rachelle Miller: The court does not always favor the woman. Often when men seek custody, they get it. In the case that they earn more money, they are in a better financial position. But both parents have a duty to support the child, regardless of who makes more money.

States won't make child support permissive—they will use wage withholding to take it out of your check. Most state courts these days have their rules written out. Judges see hundreds of cases every day with state-mandated guidelines based on a statutory formula—it's not an arbitrary dollar amount that they choose. They'll look at your income, tax statements, and number of children and plug those variables into a formula. You're not being singled out—these rules are applied across the board.

When guys complain about not seeing their children, I often find that they have taken no action with the court to get their rights enforced. There's a whole movement about father's rights, but some don't want it bad enough. They'd rather just continue the way things are. Some are content with the mother handling everything and not pressing the issue, so they've relinquished a lot of their rights.

One thing I need to get across to men is that the child support system is not their enemy; it's there to protect them, too. In crazy situations where the mother isn't allowing her child's father to see his child, he has the right to take the mother to court. The court confers your right for visitation when you are

> The child support system protects men too.

paying child support and legitimizes the payments you're making. Some men put themselves on child support. If you do this, it's important to have a third party keep a record of when you're paying.

The court will come up with a visitation schedule. A court order delineates the schedule in detail, including holidays. Provisions are made in situations where parents live more than 100 miles from each other or further. Do not let state lines deter you from seeking relief from the courts, if necessary. State agencies can work together if you and the other parent live in different states.

The Tender Years Doctrine relates to the custody of a very young child, and in the past it has been a source of perceived bias toward the mother of a child. Take for instance a case where a child is 5, and been in her mother's custody for the first four years of her life. Her father has been actively participating in her life for the past year, and he decides to take the mother to court. The court will consider the four years he was absent while the mom was doing all the rearing and nurturing. Before uprooting a child from all she has ever known, the court has to review that evidence.

The courts are reluctant to exclude either parent—you have to show great harm or abuse for the court to deny your request to have custody or terminate your parental rights. Often, courts will award joint custody. Then there's times that the child custody goes to the mother because the father doesn't want the child. It cramps the bachelor lifestyle of irresponsibility. They like their freedom to come and go as they please.

QUINCY

Hell no! Lawyers don't care about you. All they care about is how many billable hours they have. While you're fighting, you lose and the lawyer stays winning.

(John re-enters the room with a bowl of chips.)

TERRENCE

I love my children. I changed their diapers, picked them up from school... I was that guy. I wasn't a soccer dad, I was a soccer coach. I never thought I'd be in court fighting for custody of them.

During our custody battle, my ex-wife belittled me and was dishonest—said I was deadbeat. I went to friends to build alliances by divulging information I gave her in confidence. I felt very hurt and betrayed. I was hurt and lost weight. I own the home they stayed in for stability. I paid the bills and spent thousands on legal fees. In the end, the court issued an emergency injunction and awarded us shared custody.

♟ Your Rights and What You Can Do ♟

Rachelle Miller: You can come up with agreements yourself. Get something in writing from the other co-parent regarding your visitation schedule and child support payments. If you want the agreements to be legally enforceable, get them notarized. The court will honor those agreements. In the absence of a notarized agreement, the courts may enforce child support in ways that you won't like. Child support can include medical care, insurance, and day care accommodations. Guys have to understand that.

Talk to an attorney. Every state has a government unit, whether it's the Attorney General's office or it goes by another title. You can go through those agencies to work out agreements, which are enforceable by law. The services from these agencies are often at low or no cost to the person petitioning to attain child support, but many people don't avail themselves of these resources—sometimes because they are unaware they exist. But you have to do the legwork, and you have to want it bad enough.

JOHN

I'd tell women to try to work out some things outside of court. But if he's making money and he won't even give you $30 a week, take him to court. It's his obligation. He needs to try to find a way. But if he's trying to be in your child's life, don't mess with the dude.

(Terrence helps himself to some of John's chips as John pretends to snatch it away.)

♟ Man Up ♟

Dr. Page: Black men have neglected their leadership role in the family. The responsibility lies on the man if he is not in the child's life, regardless of your relationship with the mother. It's your human responsibility. The blame *is* on the man. So many of the problems discussed here are directly attributed to men being inactive in our children's lives. Mothers deal with the same issues. Regardless of job loss, racism and such, men have to be responsible for the children they create.

DJ

You gotta stay on top of that child support. Some of these young men get behind, and that's how they get you. The way it's designed and set up, it's hard. You could be laid off for seven or eight months or a year, then they send you to jail because you couldn't pay it. What sense does that make? How does that help the kid? Think about the whole situation. If he has no driver's license, he can't work. Why try to get at him then? It's unfair. And why do you have to hit me with child support if I'm already trying to help? But if you're a deadbeat, then yeah, you need to be on child support.

JOHN

Sometimes dudes feel defeated and give up. They may think, "F— it—maybe my child is better off without me." But there's other men I know who can't rub two nickels together but are still tryin' to get some ass.

(Laughter)

♟ The Wealth Killer ♟

Rachelle Miller: My final advice to men is to keep all of your children under one roof. Don't have a rainbow of baby mamas because it is a wealth killer. In the case of children with multiple mothers, there's a formula for how much money goes to each household. Of course the more children you have, the less of your check you get to keep. That's a lot of wealth coming out of your home. So be responsible when it comes to making children in the first place.

(The ladies come downstairs to see what their men are up to, talking and laughing.)

PART III: YOU AND ME AGAINST THE WORLD

CHAPTER 5

FATHER'S DAY, EVERY DAY

Everyone gathered one last time at Tony's uncle's house for the Memorial Day cookout. Most of the fellas came early to get started on the cooking. In the afternoon, the fellas left their wives, girlfriends and kids outside and gathered in the "man cave," along with Tony's uncle and some other male friends of the family. They begin to discuss how their lives have changed over the years as husbands and fathers.

Breaking the Cycle

CORY

In college, I dated this girl Tamera for two months, and she got pregnant. I had no good examples of fatherhood, all bad ones. I only have one uncle, and I saw him experience bad things with his ex-wife, including child support issues. It was terrifying to become a dad. I didn't want to go to court and have the nightmare that so many people I knew went through.

The biggest thing was telling my mother. She instilled different values in me on how to be a positive person. I didn't tell her about the baby until Tamera was eight months pregnant, and she said, "I knew already." She was my rock though—she told me we were going to get through it and do what we had to do: "You're going to be the one to change this trend in our family and break the cycle."

As a sophomore in college, I was 21 and I partied a lot. I thought life would be the same after my son was born. I had to mature. After his first birthday, I realized that if things kept going the way they were, things would be like they were with my dad. So I got a job at a movie theater—I cleaned it at night. I decided to give my all and do the right thing for my kid. It's still my motivation: I can't allow my son to feel the same way about me that I did about my dad.

Tamera took a semester off from school. I moved in with her and my son, a baby at the time. It was financially difficult to take care of them. My mother helped where she could, but I learned how far I could push myself, working two jobs and going to school. I also learned a lot about my child's mother since I didn't really know her.

Tamera never wanted me to go anywhere. One day I was gone for four hours and I came back to an empty house. She moved out! She went back to live with her mother. I was shocked but relieved. It wasn't a good atmosphere living with her.

We're at a much better place now, 13 years later. I don't have to deal with her as much now. We've had knock-down-drag-out fights yelling "I hate you" and all that, but we grew up and realized that it's not about us, it's about our son. I know what buttons not to push.

Being a father has been a great experience and reward. I have enough influence for my son to know I'm there, and that's how he carries himself. My son is mature like me, and I sometimes have to remember to hold back from telling him things that he doesn't need to know.

When I told him I was getting married, he said, "I wanna give a speech at the reception." I didn't know what he was going to say. When he spoke at the reception, he said things in his speech like, "I'm good in school... everything is because of my father." Everyone was crying... just bawling...

I did a 180. I took things for granted with my mom and what I had, but now I realize that I'm fortunate and blessed. I broke the generational curse. The curse became a blessing. My son's birth transformed my life—I committed to be better than my father. We have a better relationship than I ever had with my dad.

No Regrets

MICHAEL

I never wanted children because I had two older sisters and they had enough children for me to take care of (not that I had to). Neither of my sisters finished high school. My older sister's husband (20 years older) was in and out of jail. I knew I'd have to be a father to her kids. My other older sister met a man who was a Muslim from England, and they had two children. He disappeared—I don't know what happened. Those situations made me never want children of my own.

I have two younger brothers. I also had nephews. I felt like I had all these men to raise, like they were my own kids. Eventually I sent for my nephew. I told his father he wasn't doing his job. He's 21 and married now, with no kids, but he's smoked out every day.

My parents never talked to me about sex. I learned about sex in the streets. I went to college, joined a fraternity, studied mathematics. I had a lot of women, and the one time I had no condom, I became a father.

I love my children. Every waking moment I get I'm flying out to see them.[29] A lot of girls brought up without their fathers end up doing stupid sh—. I want to deter that. I need to show my girls that there is a man in their life that loves them. They don't need to find love with every random dude in the streets.

Funny how I go from not wanting kids to not being able to live without them. I wouldn't trade my kids for nothing in the world. I have no regrets.

---

[29] Within two weeks of this interview, Michael left Atlanta, Georgia for good and moved back home to L.A. to be close to his youngest three kids. He remains estranged from Kim as of this writing.

TERRENCE

The co-parenting arrangement with my ex-wife allows us to get along better than we did as a couple, and she's seeing something new in me now. She wouldn't like the new Terrence; she wouldn't be willing to relinquish her strong leadership style. The new Terrence wouldn't choose her.

I respect her as she is—she doesn't have to change for me; I think you should change for yourself. We don't talk about personal things, like who she's dating or where she goes to church. We have boundaries and we strictly talk about the children.

(Quincy nods.)

Taking the Lead

TERRENCE

My mom raised me to treat women the way she wanted to be treated. Chivalry was easy for me; I knew how to make a woman fall in love with me. But for most of my life, I had no father figure. I lacked leadership skills. I had to train myself to be a leader. I knew how to love a woman but not how to lead her. I've spent 20 years in corporate America, but was never a manager. I wish I had led a family and not just been the breadwinner. I failed to lead consistently. My ex-wife felt safe with me there, but she was the one coordinating vacations, and making sure bills were taken care of. In the spirit of "keeping the peace," I pretty much allowed her to take ownership of finances, and planning things. I was more casual to household and relationship issues and not taking more ownership or leadership initiatives.

> I had to train myself to be a leader.

♟ Leading in the Home ♟

Dr. Page: Ladies, work is work, but when you come home, you play house. Some women try to come home and run the house and it doesn't work. It takes cooperation, compromise—give and take.

Remember the story I gave about my daughter dating? When my wife disagreed about my decision to go inside the mall with my daughter to wait for her date, I told her, "This is my call. I know what guys are like." I was right, because the guy turned out to be late. What if I had left my daughter there by herself?

Men need to stand up and be responsible. You have to know when to assert yourself and take the initiative.

And then they get me with these fashions. My girls go shopping and bring home Spandex pants... and these shirts that don't cover girls' behinds and are too revealing. All three of them (my wife and two daughters) teamed up on me, telling me there was nothing wrong with the clothes they came home with. So next time, I went with them to Forever 21 and picked out two outfits that I deemed appropriate, instead of arguing with them about what type of clothing is considered too revealing.

Jack A. Daniels: Leadership and peace in the home all come down to three things: communication, compromise, and sacrifice.

Sacrifice says, "I won't be selfish; I will serve my partner." If we're serving each other, we care about each other's happiness. We believe in each other. I'm your best and greatest cheerleader and vice versa.

For example, let's say I'm an early bird, and my wife stays up late. If I know that, I'm going to vary my serving time to that schedule. She can give me a massage, and spend time reading with me in the evening, but I also serve her. So when I wake up the next morning, I'll get her a paper, fix the coffee, and take the kids to the bus stop.

Couples need to discuss what you think and feel, and define roles in relationship. One of you could have an assumption about roles based on your upbringing and what you've been exposed to in your relationships (such as, the man takes out the garbage and the woman does all the cooking). Teamwork makes the dream work, so if you compromise and say, "I'll let you handle that because you're better at it," it's for the best. You can't be stuck in stone age thinking like *This is a woman's place or a man's place.*

Daddy's Little Girls

PETE

I have a lot of guilt about past relationships because I did not include my daughters while I was involved with my other relationships with women. They have resented it: "You let this woman take all your time so you don't have enough time for us." They're right. I'm not thinking about getting married again because of this conflict.

TERRENCE

Part of my struggle in deciding whether to leave my wife was because of my kids. I know society's view of broken homes, not to mention my mom's struggle with me and my siblings.

In the aftermath, I had to let go of hurt. My feeling toward my children is, I can't give you a two-parent home, but I can give you an amazing guy. So I spend time with them reading, hugging them more, talking more, showing up at school more. They said, "My father is even better now." I gave them a brand new father. Sure, I could just give them money or just show up, but I really wanted to be there. I told them, "I'll never leave you or break a promise."

I'm not soft. I'm strict in some aspects, but more of a motivator and I don't yell at them. If they do something wrong, they're apologetic and ready to change before I can get on them about it.

I'm thankful for everything—the marriage, the divorce, the custody battles—because they all brought me to who I am today.

LAMAR

I don't consider myself a single father—my girls don't live with me, but I give them everything they need. I see them often. I live about a half hour away from them. As a dad, I'm not strict, but I worry about my girls a lot. I'm on edge every day if they don't call me after school. I worry about what happens at school, when they're walking home from school, and whether they are safe. I'm laid back when it comes to my son and I don't worry about him as much because I live with him. I don't get to do things with my girls like I should, or as often as I do with him.

I have a good friend who has twin daughters. We give each other feedback about what's going on in our lives and bounce things off each other.

Seen and Not Heard

TOMMY

I'm a different type of guy. There's not many of me out there. In my upbringing, I was raised to be independent. A man isn't supposed to cry. A man is supposed to take care of home and handle his business. My father is tough a guy, and my mother was tough on me too—she didn't give me no motherly type of nurturing or anything like, "Come here, let me give you a hug and make things better"; she was like, "Be a man," and "Do what you gotta do." She told me to leave her house when I was 18: "You can't stay here. I ain't takin' care of no grandbabies."[30] Things as simple as, "If you wanna drive, get your own car." Anything I got, I got it on my own. I didn't feel like I could rely on anyone to get anything.

SPENCER

My parents were married for 30 years before their divorce. My mother was a social worker, and my dad was a pastor. My parents' marriage wasn't what I thought it was. For a long time their mindset was, "You have to stay with your spouse no matter what." My mom taught me that by tolerating his cheating. So I learned that as a man, I was entitled to do whatever I want and you have to put up with it. We in the black community breed people to put up with anything, especially in the church.

> I learned that as a man, I was entitled to do whatever I want and you have to put up with it.

My grandfather had multiple women. Grandmothers turn a blind eye. They stayed with a man who was flagrant with his cheating rather than be on their own. Grandparents didn't stay together out of love—they stayed together because *they had to.*

RICO

My dad used to take me with him to go to visit his various women. He'd have me playing with the woman's child in the living room while they went in the back and did their thing. Then he'd tell me, "Don't tell your mother or you and I can't hang out no more." My dad didn't want my mother to find out and then maybe she wouldn't let him see me anymore.[31] I loved spending time with him and I looked forward to it. He was a great father.[32]

---

[30] His oldest child was born while he was in high school.

[31] Rico's parents weren't together at the time, and they were never married.

[32] His father died when he was 9 years old.

LAMAR

I haven't seen my father since 1989. I used to see my father every weekend until we moved. I was born in Antigua, and came to Brooklyn with my mother and brothers when I was 12. My father still lives in the islands. It was actually my mother who taught me how to be a man. She taught me how to do everything.

JOHN

I grew up with both parents and they were very old school. They were black-conscious and taught me that you had responsibilities—to get educated, be polite and respectful to people, and give back to the community. I was a good kid, but painfully shy—we were seen and not heard. Even if you had a valid point, an adult could shut you up and that was that. It made me more shy.

SPENCER

I didn't see my parents holding hands or kiss. They didn't talk to us. I used to be in the mall and see white parents talk

> **How can I tell a woman how I feel when I've never been allowed to say so before?**

with their children. They have conversations and allow their children to have a voice. But we don't feel like we can say things—emotionally, we're still children! How can I tell a woman how I feel when I've never been allowed to say so before?

♟ Moving On ♟

Jack A. Daniels: A lot of us didn't have father figures. It's a fact. But we gotta get over it. Don't hold onto it—it will hold you hostage. Your life will be in eternal quicksand until you let go.

A lot of men are little boys stuck in a man's body. Are you gonna repeat the cycle or break it? Cats are just whining, emotionally unstable, like "You took my toy. I didn't get what I wanted, so I'll

---

punish everyone else." That spoiled mentality is ruining our culture. Drifting from responsibility or neglecting your kids and the chance to do it right—not the way it was for you—is not the answer.

Children have questions that they can't get answers to because we're too obsessed with our own mess. Secrets keep you sick.

DEREK

If you're "Mama-ed" to death, you don't have to make a decision. You have to have manhood brought out of a man so he can walk on his own. You gotta have that brought out of you—look him in the eye and say, "You're a man." The truth of the matter is, Mama's not always gonna be there. My saving grace was that from a early age, I knew God's voice in my life.

I was five years old when my parents divorced, and I had an uncle who came around from time to time. I would glean nuggets from my grandfather and uncle.

God showed me what a man was. I had to get into the Word and say, "Who are you?" The more you walk in wisdom, power and love, the more you have, and the more you can become a man. Then you can be that for yourself and your children. Whether it's learning how to change a tire, or how to do things other guys do, like play basketball. I raised my sons alone for years. At 41, I could still be angry at my dad for not being there to teach me, or I can just go on and teach my sons. I took all the licks so they don't have to.

Role Reversal

CORY

My dad was addicted to drugs; couldn't rely on him. I saw my mother struggle. My brother is 10 years younger than me and we became the father figures in my household with my mom. My parents were only married 14 years.

PETE

My parents were married for 20 years. My dad was a drill sergeant. He was 6'2", a dominant figure, and taught me about working hard, education, travel, military and authority. Later in life my dad got mentally ill. But back in the day, I protected my mother when my father got drunk and became violent. I know one time I put him in a chokehold and my brothers had to beat me off of him. He'd do things like gamble money away, or sneak out and put his car in a ditch. So my mom looked to me for structure, with the upbringing of my siblings, bringing order to the house, and finances. It was a role reversal.

MICHAEL

I got my dad off my mom once.[33] I saw my grandfather like that but I don't know what caused it. Maria was physically violent toward me. I'm not a violent dude. She would rip out earrings, scratch me, and throw things in my face. I found out later that she dated a dude before me who used to rape her in her parents' house. So if she didn't feel loved, she'd try to bring me back in by going crazy. I left Mississippi to go back home because I didn't want either of us to go to jail and then our son would lose both his parents. I didn't want my son to see that. Everything I did helped us work it out so she could concentrate and pass the bar exam. She is a judge now.

TERRENCE

Me and my brothers were expected to be physical, as in, "Let's step outside." But I saw my mom get punched. I'd never hit a woman, even if I had to restrain her in self-defense.

---

[33] In a domestic dispute.

Trying to Be What You've Never Seen

JOE

My stepdad raised me... I didn't have a relationship with my dad. How can a 17-year-old[34] give you advice on life? Some men say the whole reason for their livelihood is to make sure their child is okay, but if you don't have that example, and all you see is hustling, what then?

If you have a kid, you know you got a responsibility bigger than yourself—not, "I want some rims." A child is more important than self-gratification. But I didn't get that because my dad had a gang of kids. My stepdad took care of us and put himself on child support... he paid $1,800 a month instead of $1,200; he had that formula. My siblings and I were good; at some point we all figure it out... You can see the difference with women who had strong fathers that raised them.

DJ

(Interjects)

True; women can respect a man and see his role in marriage, whether they were raised without a dad or not. But they can't teach a man how to be a man.

TOMMY

My parents got divorced when I was nine. My father was in the military and I can say he has always been in my life. He wasn't a deadbeat... he paid child support and we were in touch. Even though I didn't see him all the time, he was around and I didn't feel like he left me. He instilled some things in me, mostly to be tough. There was not much nurturing displayed. His attitude was,

---

[34] His father is 17 years older than him.

"You've gotta work for this and you gotta work for that. I'm not gonna give you anything." I moved in with him at a young age and he charged me rent. He talked to me about saving money but not about investing it.

I'm gifted with being able to look at situations and make my own decisions. So when I became a father, I decided I was going to do things differently. I wanted to have a better relationship with my sons. So when my oldest son came along, we were inseparable. The only reason I wasn't with my son is if I was working—I didn't run the streets. I'd purchase things for him and spent money freely for him, which is the opposite of what my father did. I gave my son more than I had. I liked to do things like going on a fishing trip with him, or doing something special as a reward for how he did on his report card. As a teen, we grew apart.

MICHAEL

My dad was never married to my mother. She left my dad to be with a dude across the street. I thought I would never go through any of that because I saw the pain my father went through. But life happens. My dad married my youngest brother's mother.[35]

My dad didn't demand to see my youngest brother even though they lived less than 10 miles apart. My brother's mother was an angry black woman. When my dad would get to the house, he'd open the door without talking to her, and my brother would walk out. Then after we all talked on the porch for a little while, he'd have to go back in the house. She never spoke to him.

I was an honor student, but my dad had no idea what was going on with me in high school. My dad didn't teach me the right things to do, so I learned from all his f—ing mistakes. He taught me to be a man by doing all the wrong things. He was a drug

---

[35] Michael has two brothers; one is four years younger and one is 12 years younger.

addict, had no teeth, used dope, and went to jail. He's the most intelligent man on this planet—but also a dumb motherf—er. His motto was, "Experience everything in life at least once... except for homosexuality." I never did drugs, but I could shoot people, rape, kill, or slap people—whatever. He opened the door for me to do anything!

I remember when he stole my $180 nugget bracelet that I got from my high school girlfriend. Then one day when I was 19, I wanted to go to the beach. My grandmother said he couldn't stay in the house. He flexes at me in the kitchen, and we go outside and square off. I'm thinking, not only does he wanna front on me in front of my people and my brother, but he's a crack head ass—always tweakin'. So I'm beating him with my class ring on my fist—his face was all bloody. My brother pulled me off him. I didn't leave Mississippi to go back home for two years after that—and we didn't talk for about three years.

On my father's side, we always hug and kiss on the cheek. He used to always say, "I got love for you," but never said he loved me. So for him not to say that, to never hug me or touch me, after a while...

(Michael shakes his head, looks down, and sighs deeply. Then he looks back up without making eye contact with anyone.)

But he's been clean now for two years. He says "I love you" and hugs me now. I don't know why. I always maintain that can't nobody say sh— about my dad because that's my dad. Even if he's wrong, I'll check him, but you can't say anything about my dad. Not even my brothers. Nobody but me.

CORY

I envisioned fathers to be like Cliff Huxtable on *The Cosby Show*, but I didn't experience that. The first and only time I saw my grandfather was at his funeral. So my father didn't have a relationship with his dad either, and my parents never talked about him.

When you're younger, you carry a lot of anger about your father not being there. I was so upset that he wasn't around. He was a union worker doing construction. He got paid on Thursday and would come home on the following Tuesday broke. He'd spend all his money in the streets. He was a functioning drug addict. My grandmother adopted kids my age. I'd be at her house playing with them (my cousins) and we'd see drug dealers and sometimes my dad would give dealers my grandmother's car for drugs and everyone knew. I couldn't get away from it, everyone knew, and it was embarrassing.

As I grew older, and started working in my organization, hearing stories and circumstances about men's issues, I realized that maybe he had his own issues that he used drugs to cope with. He wasn't close to his parents. He's been in and out of rehab since I was 10 years old. Whatever the reason is, it doesn't concern me now. I decided to get over it, accept him for who he is, but I make sure I don't do that with my son.

My brother is still dealing with anger and unforgiveness, but I had to let all that go. I just tell him to try to create better memories and let go of the anger. Where is that anger gonna get you? What am I gonna achieve? I'm a grown man and I consider myself successful. My dad doesn't owe me anything.

My dad is 66 now and still lives in Philly. I go down there to take him to his doctor appointments. He's been close to death running the streets. In this late stage of life he has transformed... his body is like an 80- or 90-year-old because of all the wear and tear from the drugs.

I just want to enjoy the time we have left with him. I can still learn some things from him. He's very intelligent—he watched and read the news, he was always informed about everything going on in the world and can have a knowledgeable conversation. I got that from him, but I stayed away from drugs. I take those as lessons learned.

Use your story as your motivation. Use your story as your motivation. You shouldn't harp on or waste your time and energy if it's not going to get you anywhere in life.

♟ When Good Role Models Are Scarce ♟

Dr. Page: When black men don't have life skills, then as soon as challenges come, they run. They don't know how to cope. Who taught them how to be men and be responsible people? Sometimes they don't have a strong father as a role model to show them that they have to stick it out when hard times come.

Jack A. Daniels: To troubled youth I say go to teachers, coaches on sports teams, and *possibly* some family members. What increases your possibilities of success is *exposure*. Join afterschool programs and look for ways to get out of the neighborhood (if it's not a positive environment). Find people who are doing something different and surround yourself with their crew. What you see plants a seed for what you can aspire to. If all you see is chaos, your mentality is going to formulate that you just need to survive. That comes at a cost of doing what's necessary just to get by.

Let's say for example that you take a kid who lives in the hood to get some gas in the suburbs. You go to pump the gas and he shouts, "What are you doing? We gotta pay for this first!" You're like, "No, it's okay," and then explain that you don't have to pre-pay for gas there. If a person is never exposed, he doesn't know that "I can't" mentality.

A Happy Blending

JOHN

I always wanted a great story. I was on Match.com looking for something romantic—I didn't want to just be with any-old-body. I wanted to be with my high school or college sweetheart. That's when love was most innocent.

I was 15 when I had my first girlfriend, and 16 when I started dating for real with a girl named Jasmyn. I dated her 'til I was 19 and we were popular at school. She was raised similar to me, and was socially aware. She was not a street chick, but a young woman. When I got to college, we broke up and stopped speaking to each other.

Anytime we saw our mutual high school friends I heard stuff like, "She hates you," and vice versa. So for the 20 years we didn't speak, we thought that we hated each other. But at a certain point, you stop giving a sh— and caring what people think. Make sure you're on good terms with folks. When you're young, you fight over dumb, petty things.

I saw Jasmyn again at a party 20 years after we broke up. I knew she was gonna be at the party.

We got married three years ago.

My wife knows who Shirley Chisholm is. I've met so many women who didn't know who she was, it's ridiculous. You ain't gotta be the next Rosa Parks. Just be knowledgeable. I can talk with my wife about Obama, current events, and politics in an intelligent conversation and we can agree to disagree. We don't have to do all the same things together.

The best part of being married is being able to chill and not worry. When my phone rings now and I'm with my wife, I'm not nervous like I used to be—I'd turn the ringer off and put the answering machine on mute. It's so refreshing for us to leave our phones on the table—I don't have to worry about some woman calling me and then I gotta act like there's no intention behind it with my wife sitting right there.

♟ Love, the Second Time Around ♟

Dr. Utley: Parents should be respectful of each other. I think they should definitely let the co-parent meet the new partner before he or she moves in with the family. Co-parents don't get a say about who their partner dates, but they should be informed.

Often couples break up because they fail to grow together. After a split, people are free to grow at their own pace and sometimes find themselves compatible with a former partner. At times it works, at other times, it only appears as if there's compatibility. The idea of being together is more seductive than the practicality of being together.

Jack A. Daniels: Playing house is never good for the child. They are very aware of the emotions in their external environment. It presents a false idea of happiness. They start to think men or women pretend, then they leave. Prepare the children and let them know if you're severing ties. It creates more confusion when parents start dating (others, or each other) and they're still in the same house, "separated."

Trina Proctor: It is important for the two biological parents involved to set aside their personal differences that led to them separating or remarrying for the sake of any kids involved. It is necessary to have a conversation with the children of all ages with some sort of mediator about the decisions being made to separate or remarry. There have been many families destroyed and children in difficult situations due to a lack of communication. Some parents feel as though "My child is just 3 or 7, they are too young to understand what is going on." Children deserve an explanation about why their life is being disrupted or altered.

Children of all ages need to know that stepparents and biological parents are a "united front" when it comes to discipline and setting moral standards. This involves communication and compromise on all ends. If the children of blended families and stepfamilies know that they are not able to run to another party in the family to avoid discipline and living up to household standards, they will achieve the majority of the expectations set by their parents. This will avoid confusion for everyone!

CORY

I got married to Jessica last year. We've only been together three years, but we've known each other since age 10. My stepson (her son) Kevin is seven. Jessica and his father, Dave, were previously engaged for seven years.

It was my son who told me that his mother's boyfriend moved in, not her. I wanted to meet him and discuss expectations. I wasn't mad about the situation because I moved on, but I need to know who's living with my son.

Having a blended family is a sensitive thing. I had to adjust to Kevin. His dad is a good guy and they have a good relationship. I talked to Dave about my relationship with Kevin. I wanted Dave to know that I wasn't trying to take his place as Kevin's father. He was reluctant to talk with me because he still had feelings for Jessica. They were broken up for a year before we got together, but you know men don't appreciate what they have until it's gone. We are respectful to each other and I reassured him that everything would be good between all of us. I didn't want to use his son as a pawn and make him feel uncomfortable or disloyal.

I stay out of Jessica and Dave's issues—it's not my place when it comes to their son for me to butt in. Of course if she asks, I'll give her my opinion as her husband and as a father. We're not the Brady Bunch, but we have an understanding.

CHAPTER 6

BRINGING IT ALL HOME

By all accounts, environmental, political, and social factors in American society make life challenging for black men to say the least. What do we need to do in the black community to help ourselves be better and do better?

Role Modeling in the Home

MELISA ALABA

The major thing to focus on when it comes to parenting is role modeling our relationships. The behavior children see will repeat itself in their lives positively or negatively. If kids see parents in a bad relationship, using poor communication, talking negatively about each other, screaming and using profanity with each other, the kids grow up with feelings of abandonment that they can't express, so they carry it with them for years.

We have to have stronger families together. If more black families were married, our kids would be better off. We need a moral foundation and guidelines for when we have relationships without being married. We need to teach our children how to date, and how men and women should interact with each other. If kids see proper relationships in the home, it doesn't matter what they see on TV—they'll do better in school and have a good foundation of social wellness and interaction. Seeing and experiencing proper relationship interactions gives them safety, and builds their selflessness (instead of selfishness).

Leaving a Legacy

ZEKE

We can leave a legacy either by design or by default (if we do nothing).

My last name is a recognizable brand. Our community has confusion on how to build a strategy to make a brand that represents their family; a brand we can pass on to our children and not be ashamed of.

Multigenerational family issues impact our culture and make us feel like failures. TV, magazines and newspapers are causing us to stumble. Blind spots may exist in our family that affect how we live now. They impact us but we're not always sure what it was; you just pick up on things that become habits.

Every ounce of my being says that I want to pass to my children a life well lived.

Do you know how to build a life based on what you want your legacy to be? We have to show ourselves to be fully present in the lives of our children. It's a heart issue. If the heart is not convinced that something is wrong, the desire to change things is not prioritized.

You have to be bold and approach things. You will come against opposition whenever there's change.

Some supportive concerns may arise. Decide to have family loyalty and enhance your reputation collectively. Give age-appropriate responsibilities to each family member. Validate the women. Establish the proper hierarchy from parents to children (we're not friends, we're your parents). Adopt the attitude that when one of us succeeds, we all succeed.

JACK

Some of us are wasting time in mazes of bewilderment on our own. Some women waste the best years of their lives with men who ain't never gonna get it together.

What do we stand to lose? We lose ourselves. We lose where we came from. We can lose the great qualities our culture has, and we lose our identity. And if you lose direction, you lose purpose. If you lose purpose, what are you doing?

We have to prevent all of this by coming together. A legacy is at stake. To create a legacy requires a team.

Seventy percent of blacks are raised in single parent households. With so many unwed blacks, we're losing family. We have to get back to basics. Relationships are the foundation of community, and community is the foundation of culture.

There's way too many selfish people. If you worry about yourself, you end up by yourself. Understand that there's more to life than your selfish ambitions.

One of my clients is getting divorced in her 50s. She said, "Should I settle for being comfortable, or die alone? Who's gonna want me?" Her biggest fear is dying alone.

Another client I have hates her mother, whom she is taking care of. She resents that her mother never took care of her when she was a child. She's ready to walk away from her ill mother, but if she does, her mother could go to a nursing home and die alone.

What's the point of life if you have no one to share it with; if you have nothing to show for your life but a bunch of broken promises and dreams, women you've taken advantage of, and children you've neglected?

Our problem is, we do not acknowledge the things we're doing now and the impact it will have on our future. We must be prideful of who we are and the legacy we will leave in this world.

AFTERWORD

'**ve learned so much from each of the 16 men I interviewed for this book. For one thing, I learned that men DO talk. They just need an environment where they can open up fully and know that the other person will listen without interrupting, criticizing, or berating them for their thoughts and opinions. They have emotions, disappointments, fears, aspirations, hopes and dreams just like anyone else, and as Jack explained, they are much more sensitive than women (quiet as it's kept). They felt free to speak to me and let their guards down. Some even considered it to be like therapy and wanted to talk much longer than the scheduled allotted time. I'm honored that each of them were forthcoming enough to be honest about what's really going on in their relationships, their hang-ups, and what they need from us as women.

My hope is that the conversations and advice in this book have given you some insight to the struggle of black men in becoming good fathers and partners to black women, as well as tools that you can use in your current or future romantic relationships.

What will you do now?

How will you use the information in these pages to improve your relationships? Let's build together and heal hurting black families. It's up to us. Hit me up at DareeAllen.com and leave a comment about the insights you've learned from this book, and tell me about the legacy you want to leave for your family.

ACKNOWLEDGMENTS

God is first in my life. God gave me the ability to write, and the heart to love it. Thank You for Your grace; You gave me a positive outlet to turn dating discouragement into something constructive for the masses.

Rico, I thank you for bringing me the idea for this book. Although I'm not happy about the reasons that inspired it, I thank you for sharing your truth. Grandma and Grandpa would be proud of us.

To all of the "characters" in this book—the guys who let me get in their personal business: Although you will remain anonymous here, I see you! Thank you for allowing me and other women to get a glimpse into your lives, and to the plights and struggles of black men everywhere. Even though I don't know most of you personally, I feel like I know you. I enjoyed each and every interview, and I wish you much success in life and love. On behalf of black women, I can tell you sincerely: We need you. I believe this book is going to help many who are, or who have been where you've been.

To Myles and all of my expert contributors, I thank you for your time, analysis, and enlightening commentary.

To the staff of BookLogix, for easing the stress of designing this work and helping me bring it to fruition.

ABOUT THE AUTHOR

Daree Allen, MS is a technical writer and motivational youth speaker. As a vocal introvert, her favorite activities outside are teaching TurboKick (kickboxing) and Hip Hop Hustle, and dancing (especially line dances); her favorite inside activity is to chill at home or with friends. Daree resides in Atlanta, Georgia with her daughter, Kaia, and she's probably online right now. You can find her at:

http://DareesInsights.wordpress.com

http://DareeAllen.com.

www.ingramcontent.com/pod-product-compliance
Lightning Source LLC
Chambersburg PA
CBHW060539100426
42742CB00013B/2392